EXPLORE
YOUR
INNER SELF

EXPLORE
YOUR
INNER SELF

Dilys Hartland

CAXTON REFERENCE

© 2000 Caxton Editions

This edition published 2000 by Caxton Editions,
20 Bloomsbury Street, London, WC1B 3QA.

Caxton Editions is an imprint of the Caxton Publishing Group.

Printed and bound in India .

CONTENTS

Chapter 1 INTRODUCTION

Know thyself   9

Having it all   14

The blame culture   22

Drugs – a way out   24

Sigmund Freud and the quest for the inner self   27

'The unexamined life is not worth living'   32

Chapter 2 LOOKING OUTSIDE FOR INNER ANSWERS

Health check   39

Psychotherapy   45

Client-centered counselling   50

Gestalt therapy   53

Transactional analysis   58

Cognitive therapy   71

Inner child therapy   77

Counselling for a specific event   83

Time out   85

Retreats   93

Self-help through books and groups   98

Religion   103

Personality type 109

The Myers-Briggs Type Indicator 114

Type A and Type B personalities 117

Chapter 3 THE PSYCHIC PLANE

Palmistry 128

Astrology 130

Chapter 4 DEVELOPING YOUR INNER RESOURCES

Yoga 138

The Alexander technique 142

Aromatherapy 148

Reading 153

Write your way to wisdom 155

Expanding the mind 159

Meditation 165

Dream interpretation 173

Death: the final frontier 183

Chapter 5 FAMILY HISTORY

Tracing our roots 187

Adoption 201

Further Reading 213

Useful Addresses 219

CHAPTER 1

INTRODUCTION

*Man is a being which consists not so much
in which it is, as in what it is going to be.*

[José Ortega y Gasset, 1883–1955]

For the purposes of this book, the self is defined
as being a whole made up of three entities:
mind (that is, intellect: the brain which we use
to organise and function in the world, and
interpret the world to ourselves); body; and
spirit (our inner selves, made up in itself of
many complex layers of conscious and
unconscious understanding).

The three parts make up an indivisible
whole, and they interact constantly with each
other. Bodily health or bodily illness exert a
powerful influence over the mind; a life lived
entirely in the mind is starved both of the joys

of the body and the richness of the spirit or inner self – which in turn can lead to bodily sickness. The creative and wide-ranging spirit needs to be anchored in the real world by mind and body.

This book is an introductory guide for those who wish to explore their inner selves. In a world which increasingly seems to threaten and confuse, our inner selves are the one sure thing we can rely on; the one certain resource we can develop, and in which we can find happiness and fulfilment.

Know thyself

These words – in the ancient Greek – were inscribed on the temple of Apollo at Delphi hundreds of years before the birth of Christ and the beginning of what we call the first millenium.

It may seem to us now that the ancient Greeks were not the fragmented personalities we can feel ourselves to be today. A man could be – was expected to be –not only cultured and educated, knowledgeable about music and the arts, but an athelete, a sportsman, a soldier able and willing to defend his city or state. He would take part in the political life of his society; he would practice the religion of that society, and have an interest in philosophical debate. We'd be right to envy this well-rounded person leading such a full life – knowing as we do now, however, that such a privileged life was led only by a few and all of those were men, that women were excluded, and that the fabric underpinning this apparently ideal society was slavery.

As the twentieth century grew to a close, it

seemed a natural time for reflection, for looking back to see how far we had come, and to look forward with optimism, curiousity and perhaps not a little fear as well. The dawn of each new year is naturally a time of personal reflection and assessment.

Quoting Charles Dickens, we can say that it's the best of times, and the worst of times. In Britain at least, we no longer hang criminals in public or send small boys up chimneys; children do not work long hours in factories, and their safety and wellbeing is protected by numerous laws. Our hospitals are free, and we live longer, healthier lives. Generally speaking, most of us have more than enough food, live in comfortable homes, and reap enough financial reward from our daily work to be able to afford clothes, cars, holidays, luxuries, all the 'toys' of contemporary life.

We can watch *Oliver Twist* or *David Copperfield* on television, or any other historical drama, and be thankful not to live in such a world, where poverty led to the workhouse and misfortune to a debtors' prison.

And yet, and yet…however good life may be

for some of us, we know that the world is still a terrible place. In the last few months alone, the TV screen and the daily paper have brought terrifying images from Chechnya, from Kosovo, from India, from Venezuela – images of natural catastrophe, and of man's overwhelming inhumanity to man. Planes fall from the sky, trains collide, cars crash with devastating consequences: is there anywhere we can feel truly safe?

There have been wars on this planet almost from the day human beings started to walk upright, and natural disasters are beyond our control. But there are two factors that seem particularly to distinguish this time in the life of our planet. One is that more people fear personal violence than in earlier times. Fortunately murder in Britain is still a comparatively rare crime compared with, say, the United States but the apparent statistics on crimes like rape, mugging and racist or homophobic assaults rightly make us uneasy. Like the TV cop used to say, you have to be careful out there. And we have all become aware of the random act of violence – Dunblane, to give just one terrible example; what could be more natural, normal or everyday than a school hall full of bright shining young faces? What kind of world is it in which such horror can destroy dozens of lives in a matter of seconds?

The second factor is our physical environment, this beautiful planet on which we live and which has supported life so easily and lavishly for so long. Every day we are made aware of the ways in which our super-abundant lifestyles are affecting this earth. By owning refrigerators, driving cars and centrally heating our houses, we are contributing to the greenhouse gases which we are told are unravelling the ozone layer like a ladder in a pair of tights, causing water levels to rise and fall with potentially alarming consequences. Just by living our normal everyday lives – having a bath, driving to work, sitting in a heated well-lit office, buying sandwiches wrapped in plastic for lunch and drinking Coke out of a plastic bottle or a throwaway tin, reading a newspaper, looking at holiday brochures and planning a plane trip to some pleasant location – all of these activities, we're told, create mess and pollution and one day we are just going to be buried under the piles of our own rubbish.

And what's the truth of all this? Are we doomed, as some of the scientists and experts and environmental campaigners would have us believe? Or can we somehow stop the rot and reverse what seems an inevitable process of decay and destruction? More importantly, what can we as individuals do to stop feeling so helpess, so powerless to save our planet and protect our children's children?

Having it all

During the 1980s and 1990s, it seemed there was a growing divide between the kind of lives we should be living, and our actual experience of those lives.

These were the years of 'having it all' and that 'it' could be defined almost exclusively in terms of money, consumption, buying, owning, using.

Men in our high-tech Western culture were expected to be successful high achievers, their careers moving upwards and onwards to higher salaries, bigger expense accounts, flashier cars. This was the age of the yuppy, of the mobile phone, the man on the move. The mobile phone came, in fact, to symbolise the age: a man so busy, so in demand, so important, that he could not go anywhere where he could not be instantly contacted by the people so dependent on him. A man whose life was one of such hectic and relentless activity that he had to have his phone with him at all times because he would never be in one place long enough.

The reality, however, was somewhat different. Just as the apparent glamour and importance of the mobile phone is more usually reduced to the banality of a man on a train calling someone to say 'I'm on the train', so this high-achieving lifestyle hid other realities. The suicide rate among men rose; almost everyone knows someone who has a friend who simply dropped dead at forty of a heart attack. As markets worldwide became more competitive, pressures in the workplace increased. From the 1970s onwards, companies merged with other companies in their bid to secure ever-larger slices of the market cake, and jobs were shed. Men who thought they could amply provide for their families for life found themselves redundant at 48 and unlikely ever to work again, at least not at the level or in the capacity which they had foreseen.

The introduction of information technology meant workers had to learn more, do more, and faster. Employers thought that one computer system equalled five or ten jobs; though in practice that often meant that ten people were discarded, and the remaining five still did the same amount of work as before. In the Japanese language, a word came to exist for 'death by overwork'.

Women, meanwhile, having been 'liberated' in the 60s by the contraceptive pill and the Women's Liberation Movement, were free to move out of the kitchen, the nursery and the bedroom into the 'real' spheres of life. Indeed, they were almost expected to – the career woman became an ideal, the housewife-and-mother of yesteryear a discarded model. Trouble is, it didn't quite work out like that. Women wanted careers and were glad to have them, but they also wanted babies and marriages. Somehow, statistics have shown, women still end up being solely responsible for the ironing, the shopping, the housework, the 3 a.m. feeds. If they also happen to have a 9a.m. meeting with an important client, then that just adds to the rich tapestry of their lives.

So we ended up in a muddle. The career woman idealised by *Cosmopolitan* and other glossy magazines may have had a glamorous job in fashion, the media or the City – almost undoubtedly she also had a live-in nanny. For many women, in far more ordinary jobs, juggling children and a job meant rushing to the child-minder's at 7.45 a.m., rushing to work, rushing to collect the baby at 5.30 p.m. leaving an in-tray approaching Everest proportions, feeling equal amounts of guilt and frustration at being both a 'bad' mother and a 'bad' employee.

Men didn't have it any easier in their personal lives in the later half of the twentieth century. Having spent the better half of two millenia being Masters of the Universe – warriors, rulers, breadwinners, decision makers, Paterfamilias – they suddenly found, in the matter of a decade or so, that superior position challenged and themselves in some cases (literally) redundant. If a woman can earn £60,000 a year, pay her own mortgage, employ a nanny for her children, does she really need a husband? The old order – where women stayed at home and men worked – was largely based on the economic principle that poorly educated women could not get the high-flying jobs men could. Once that changed, everything else did.

In the under-privileged sections of society, the redundancy of men became a terrifying fact in every sense of the word. On the housing estates of Britain, the ghettoes of the unemployed and unemployable, a new class of young male grew up. Disenfranchised from birth, growing up in poverty, he grew up in a world where he knew there were no jobs, no work, no future available for him. An important part of the male psyche in our culture has always been their ability to work, to provide, to feed and clothe their children. We expect it of them, and they expect it of themselves. For generations, this is how men have defined themselves. Suddenly, that was no more. Even worse, their girlfriends and women survived: because they had children, they were given council accommodation and state benefits. If the state would provide for them, why would they need men? This depressing cycle of deprivation, low expectations and an invisible future has led to the kind of mindless violence that is born of frustration and brick wall horizons.

The decades of the 80s and 90s were decades of high stress, high unemployment, job insecurity, and personal debt. No longer do people have the security of jobs for life:

redundancy, with all the emotional and financial consequences of that, became a fact of life for many.

The introduction of the credit card ('your flexible friend') meant that we need never save up for anything ever again. We really could have it all, now, today. This was an innovation which crucially separated us from the cautious, thrifty attitude of our parents. My father, for example, was born in 1903. He worked for the same company all his life until retirement. It never occurred to him to change his job because he liked what he did and he felt a strong sense of loyalty to his employers, and gratitude to them for employing him. He had been a young man in the 30s; unemployment (in a world before state benefits) was a nightmare to him. He earned a reasonable salary, but he had two very strong ethical principles where money was concerned: a need to save for his old age, and a horror of debt. My father was not without the consumer durables of his time – he owned a car just as soon as car-owning became a possibility for the 'ordinary' man, he owned a record player, and later on a TV; my mother had a twin-tub washing machine – but the difference between then and now is that all these items were paid for cash on the nail, paid for before they left the shop or the showroom.

Growing up as I did in the late 50s and 60s, I found his attitudes stodgy and boringly out of date. Post-war Britain was a grey, dull place. Britain had won the war, and yet we seemed somehow to be losing the peace. I had grown up with austerity, 'making do', 'saving your pennies' and 'saving for a rainy day' – the revolution of the 1960s signified an altogether happier, more colourful, less restricted world. But still we weren't happy.

The credit card boom of the Thatcher years seemed a natural extension of such joyfulness. At last the drudgery of the post-war years was finally erased by a have-it-now culture.

It seems as if our parents may have been right after all. The spending sprees of the 80s and 90s, combined with job insecurity and an economy in deep recession, led to high levels of personal debt never before seen.

'Stress' became the most commonly used five-letter word, the designer disease of the 90s:

Stress at work, where it seemed that people worked longer hours, had less security, and missed out on family life and personal relationships because of the demands of these jobs; stress is our personal lives, as the divorce rate in Britain became the highest in Europe and it seemed as if family life and enduring relationships were a thing of the past.

Hygiene and health technologies have meant that the killer diseases of the past such as cholera and typhus have disappeared in Western countries. Tuberculosis, once all-but-conquered, is making a frightening reappearance among the poor and malnourished. But by and large, however, we are healthier and live longer than our National Health Service can provide for us, and the biggest killers are stress and lifestyle-related diseases such as heart disease and cancer.

The blame culture

One response to the apparent chaos of the world is to look for someone to blame. This disturbing trend is of pandemic proportions in the US, where the 'ambulance chasing' lawyer is a feature of contemporary life. If you are ill, if your marriage fails, if your child is killed in a car crash or some other catastrophe – sue someone.

This is not to excuse those occurrences which truly are the result of negligence and where the facts must be made known in order to guard against a re-occurrence, and this is not to deny those deprived of a breadwinner the right to fair compensation.But underlying the blame culture is a refusal to accept the world as it is. There's a book and a song with the same title: I never promised you a rose garden. The world has never been safe or cosy, and dreadful things happen. Sometimes we can learn from events, and resolve to change the world a little as a result.

We should also take personal responsibility for our lives, our joys and sorrows, and understand that looking for a scapegoat does not dull or soften the pains and the tragedies of real life.

It's no accident that the blame culture has developed so fully in the US, the country that gave us Hollywood. Hollywood is a fabulous confection, a make-believe, a fantasy world of happy endings, of boy-gets-girl, of the good guy winning and the bad guy losing, of love conquering all and the final triumph of justice. Movies enrich our lives immeasurably, entertaining, instructing and diverting. But they are not the same as real life, and it's the most dangerous fantasy of all to believe that they do.

Drugs – a way out

Another phenomenon of our time is the drugs culture. There's nothing particularly new about this. As long as humans have been on the planet, they have sought out substances to smoke, eat or – more commonly perhaps – to drink which have dulled pain, elevated mood and altered consciousness. In Britain, as in other countries, our ancestors drank at rates we consider excessive today: before the widespread introduction of tea and coffee, and in the days before clean drinking water was widely available, most people began the day with beer or wine. Anyone who thinks too much alcohol is consumed today should read social histories of the eighteenth or nineteenth centuries; for the poor in those days, gin was a cheap and plentiful way out of immediate distress.

The desire to enhance a happy occasion, to lubricate a social event or simply to give one's mood a lift is entirely natural, and we should ignore the prudes who say otherwise. But addiction to drugs of any kind – whether it's an unemployed teenager in Glasgow hooked on heroin, a City whizkid snorting cocaine or a bored housewife on her third bottle of chardonnay – are a symptom, and until we look at the reason why that person needs that drug we will never find solutions to the problem. And it is a problem: the drugs trade, the use of drugs, the mis-use of alcohol are behind many of the deeply disturbing elements in our society – petty crime, not-so-petty crime, domestic violence, the alarming prospect of gang warfare on a large scale.

A heroin addict once described the chain of events that led her to the drug. She had moved from home to a big city, and knew no one. Her home life has not been good and she did not have a support network of family and friends to fall back on. Desperately lonely and insecure, she described how her first-ever hit of heroin made her feel wonderful: 'It was like being wrapped up in love', she said, 'I felt safe inside this big warm blanket of good feelings'. Tragically, her need for these good feelings, and her inability to get them for herself in any other way, led to a long and debilitating dependence on the drug and the familiar patterns of stealing to pay for it, health breakdown, seeking the company of other addicts, and neglecting her own safety and wellbeing. The road back from such a hell is long and hard, and many don't make it.

Sigmund Freud and the quest for the inner self

Sigmund Freud (1856–1939) is known as the father of psychoanalysis: that is, he was the first thinker to attempt to map what is inside us in a way which combined science with art, medical fact with spiritual insight.

Freud today is a controversial figure, and there are many who criticise his theories and his approach. In the 1960s, for instance, feminists found intolerable his theory that women suffer from penis envy. It was pointed out that Freud lived and worked among the privileged upper classes of nineteenth-century Vienna, and based his theories on what he observed among this very small section of a society that is hardly representative. But psychoanalysis moves on and develops, and were Freud alive today he would undoubtedly want to develop or even abandon many of his own theories. (Nobody criticises Henry Ford for not producing the Aston Martin.)

One area in which this is so is sexuality. Freud saw sex as the driving force behind men; he said he did not know what women wanted, a disarming admission which probably reveals as much about Freud the man as about anything else. Today, interpreters of Freud and other psychoanalysts tend to see sex as a metaphor – that is, it may not be sex itself that men want (although in many instances of course it is) but what sex can seem to represent: namely, power.

Anybody who seeks to find out something about their inner lives will come into contact with Freud's theories. Freud described the inner self as being composed of layers – what for convenience is now called the conscious and the unconscious. He described:

The Id – our 'deep unconsciousness' made up of basic needs or drives: the drive for food, or warmth, or sex. The latter is important in Freud, as he thought that most neuroses (that is, psychological imbalance) arose from repressed or disturbed sexuality.

The Superego – our 'conscience', which controls or forbids the expression of drives.

The Ego – the conscious mind, which acts as a sort of control centre, balancing the varying commands of Id and Superego.

This is obviously a simplistic reduction of a very complex area, but Freud's contribution was to see the inner self not as one conscious whole, but as made up of many conflicting levels of awareness. The inner life drives our conscious actions, negatively as well as positively.

A key theory in Freud is repression. Unpleasant or shameful feelings or memories are locked away in the unconscious, leading either to neurosis or to physical illness (what we now call psychosomatic illness). The role of repression can be illustrated by three examples:

1. We all have angry feelings: anger is a protective, healthy part of our make up. A parent who forbids a child to display anger is driving that anger into the unconscious. A deep anger builds up inside that child, an anger which is allowed no normal form of expression. In the adult, it may reveal itself either as depression or as 'explosions' of uncontrollable rage which seem out of all proportion to the incident which triggered it. In more extreme cases, schizophrenia may develop.

2. An alcoholic parent may create a home

environment which is chaotic and muddled. In seeking to escape this, a super-tidy child grows up, one who may be neat and organised to the point of obsession-compulsion. Interestingly, as an adult that child may choose a partner who is either alcoholic or chronically untidy or both. This devastasting choice – with unhappy consequences for all – is because in his or her unconscious that child needs the chaos which is their earliest and strongest memory of home.

3. Freud described what he called conversion hysteria and we know as psychosomatic illnesses. Patients develop very real physical symptoms to handle 'psychic overload'. Examples of this which Freud himself saw were men who were shell-shocked during World War I. Unable consciously to deal with the horrors they had seen, they developed physical conditions (blindness, for example, or paralysis). In today's society we may point to eating disorders as examples of this syndrome: the patient retreats into a situation whereby they exert excessive control over their food intake as a means of dealing with their inability to control other events in their lives.

Freud, like his co-worker Jung, was passionately interested in dreams. Nothing, he believed, is accidental, and least of all our dreams, which represent the direct voice of our unconscious mind.

Further Reading

Sigmund Freud, The Essentials of Psychoanalysis, Penguin.

Freud for Beginners, Richard Osborne, Writers and Readers Paperback.

Sigmund Freud, The Interpretation of Dreams, Editor Angela Richards, Penguin.

The Freud Reader, Editor Peter Gay, Penguin.

'The unexamined life is not worth living'

So wrote the Greek philosopher Socrates, and that philosophy is the purpose of this book. Many of us feel the need to try and make some sense of the world around us, and the only place we can really start is within ourselves.

We can't change the world, and we may not really want to change ourselves either. But in acquiring a measure of self-understanding we come to like ourselves better, to see ourselves as whole people, to respect ourselves as travellers on that human journey towards death that is inevitable for all of us.

We're not alone on that journey of self-discovery – there is much that can help and support us on the way. This book describes, very briefly, some of them.

Here is an exercise to start you thinking about the 'furniture' of your interior life.

Sit quietly and undisturbed, with a big sheet of plain paper (minimum size A4) in front of you. Across the centre of this paper, draw a dotted line. At the left-hand end of this dotted line, put the date of your birth: 25 May 1960. At the right-hand end put the date of your tenth birthday: 25 May 1970.

Don't spend too long thinking, but using the middle line as the base draw a dotted line above and below for the highs and lows of those ten years as you remember them. Draw a little diagram or write in a word or two what the event was.

For instance, if the birth of a brother or sister was a high point, take your dotted line above the central line and either draw a picture of a baby or write your sister's name (and of course if this event was a trauma or an upset for you, take your line below the central line and do the same).

In this way, plot an emotional graph of your first ten years in words and pictures. Don't include things you think you should be important; if starting school was no big deal, leave it out. If finding a huge spider in your bed was a horror that still chills you, draw a very **big** spider below the central line. Everyone thinks they ought to remember 'significant' events like Auntie Annie's wedding, but as a small child you may have found a particular visit to the cinema or the circus more moving and memorable.

The point of this exercise is to focus on you as a young child, less than ten years old. Let what memories you have come naturally to the surface of your mind. If no memories come, is there a reason? Have you perhaps 'lost' some memories because they are too painful to explore? Can you recall the feelings of those years – were you generally cheerful, silent, noisy or happy? In exploring your inner self, you have to go right back to the beginning and look at your earliest years, and the child that you were (and in many ways, still are). You have grown, been educated, taken your place in the world, become an adult: but it is absolutely certain that nothing has shaped you as much as the events of those first few years. This is because you were physically small, and inexperienced in the ways of the world, and very very vulnerable. You absorbed like a sponge all hat was said and done to you.

When you have finished with your dotted line, spend a few moments brain-storming on the reverse of the sheet of paper. Write down everything that comes to mind about those first ten years. Nobody will see this paper, so it does not have to be explanatory, nor does it have to be logical. You know that association 'game' that psychiatrists are supposed to be so fond of, where the psychiatrist says a word and the patient says the first word that comes into her head? It's like that, only the word is 'Childhood' and what you write may be something like this:

Rice pudding on Fridays – the smell of my grandmother – Dad going into hospital to have his appendix out – anger anger anger anger – the dog run over outside the house – wetting my pants at Sarah's wedding – losing one of my new shoes on the way home – the frightening man who followed me in the park – sitting-room wallpaper – Dr Who on telly on a Saturday – I hate Jackie – crying in arithmetic lessons -

Keep this piece of paper, and look at it again in six months' time. Later on, you may want to repeat the exercise for the years between ten and twenty, and so on.

Chapter 2
LOOKING OUTSIDE FOR INSIDE ANSWERS

'The journey of a thousand miles begins with a single step.'

For some, the journey to self-awareness is precipitated by a crisis. A life event, often a bereavement or loss of some kind, throws us into inner turmoil and we begin to question every aspect of our lives – who am I? What do I believe in? Why did this happen to me?

Depression – that illness-without-a-name until recent times – can be another trigger. There does not always have to be a 'cause' for depression, although of course personal circumstances can lead to a bout of depression.

The depressed person feels life is being lived at one remove; you go through the motions of daily life without really being there, unable to think or feel or enjoy as you would wish. The depressed person is somehow separate from themselves, and in an effort to integrate themselves, to feel whole again, they are drawn to therapy with the aim of getting in touch with themselves.

Health check

As with any other kind of journey, it's wise to check up on your own personal health before setting out.

An important part of exploring ourselves is to realise that we are a whole person, that is, body and mind and spirit are all integral parts of the same being. We all know people who emphasise one at the expense of another: the health-and-fitness freak who totally ignores the relationships in his life, or a worthwhile career; the academic who lives so much inside his or her own head that they become ill through neglect of the body.

If you begin your journey from a low point and feel that you may be suffering from clinical depression, see your doctor. It may be that a short course of drug therapy can help: depression can make the sufferer too ill to help themselves. By inducing a sense of wellbeing, the right drug can make you feel like helping yourself further.

Much is heard these days about, for example, *Prozac* (fluoxetine) and its beneficial effects on depressive illness. It may indeed be, as some medical researchers claim, that depression is actually much more of a physical illness than anyone realised, and that by altering certain chemicals in the brain the condition can be cured.

There's no definitive answer on that yet. But if you are seriously depressed, don't hesitate to talk to your doctor and take advice.

Our genes predispose us to certain types of illness or condition, and if you suffer from some specific medical condition then you will want to take all the help the medical profession can offer. But to a great extent – and this will be true for the majority of people – our health lies within our own control. In choosing not to smoke, for instance, or in choosing to quit if you do, you are making a major decision affecting your future health.

Almost anything in life seems easier to cope with if we are physically fit. How often have you heard people say 'Well, at least I've got my health?' Without health we cannot work, or plan, or fully enjoy the world, or take responsibility for our own lives.

This is a self-help world, and bookshops, health-food stores and magazine racks are groaning under the weight of diet books and magazines. The advice given is diverse and often bewilderingly contradictory. Every week there is some new fad or fashion concerning food, diet and exercise and, as with most fashions, sooner or later they all fade away.

If you are a fit and healthy person, it is probably because you are following some of the simple rules outlined below. If you are not as healthy as you would like to be, then this seems to be what you need to do:

● If you smoke, give it up. There is nothing good to be said about the habit, which is expensive and just plain bad for you and the others who share your space. It may be hard to stop, but you're not alone – the world is full of reformed smokers who will sympathise and offer support, and there are local and national helplines too. Look in *Yellow Pages* or *Thomson's*, or ask in your doctor's surgery.

● The same applies if you regularly use illegal

drugs (and apart from alcohol they all are). Don't trash yourself if you have needed this kind of crutch; but it is a crutch, and you deserve better for yourself.

● If you regularly drink too much, cut down to sensible, manageable levels. If you think you may have a problem with drinking, talk in confidence to someone who can help you. Try to have as many alcohol-free days during the week as you can (which does not mean bingeing at the weekends).

● Eat less sugar, salt, sweet and sticky foods, hot and spicy foods.

● Eat more fruit, fresh vegetables and complex carbohydrates such as pasta and wholemeal bread.

● If you think you are overweight, eat what you like, but less of it.

● Take up a regular form of exercise. The only worthwhile exercise is something you enjoy, because that way you will stick at it and make it a feature of your life. A brisk half-hour walk in the fresh air every day is every bit as good (and cheaper) as hours at the gym or squash club.

The benefits of exercise extend to all the areas of your life. 'A healthy mind in a healthy body', the Romans said; exercise gives us the chance to reflect, to think, to enjoy being in our bodies.

The writer Leslie Kenton, who has written many insightful books on diet and health, wrote that if trying to lose weight we should imagine ourselves as a block of marble on which a sculptor is working. The craftsman creates a work of art from what he has to work with, smoothing and shaping and bringing to life the innate perfection of that material.

The message is an important one, especially in this celebrity-crazy world of ours. The aim of cherishing your physical self is to make it as good as it can be – but when you go swimming or to the gym, or walking, it is your body that's important; not the body of whoever the supermodel or rock star of the moment is.

We live in a society dominated by movie and

magazine images, and we compare ourselves unfavourably with celluloid creations. To many teenage girls, for instance, the phrase *'I'm not beautiful'* actually means *'I don't look exactly like Victoria Beckham'*. We are not encouraged to value ourselves as individuals – whatever we look like. The road to self-discovery is not about turning ourselves into copies of someone else: it is about finding out who we ourselves, unique individual and irreplaceable, really are.

Psychotherapy

Restoration of the freedom to change is the goal of treatment

For many, self-awareness may begin with a course of psychotherapy. For others, it is part of the process. There are many different types of psychotherapy, a few of which are briefly described below, but the aim of all of them is to increase the individual's sense of self. It is easier to say what psychotherapy is not, in fact, than to say what it is.

First of all, it won't 'solve' your problems. Some people, indeed, find that it creates new ones – opening the Pandora's box of the past requires courage and commitment, and things may often lie buried deep in our psyche which are painful to look at in the cold light of day. A therapist will offer support and companionship on the journey, but they cannot make the journey for you.

Second, no therapist worth their fee should tell you what to do. If you hear a therapist using words like 'you must' or 'you ought' then I advise you to question whether or not you are seeing the right person. The therapist is there to listen attentively, to focus on you and the story you have to tell. They may encourage, suggest, guide, offer comment occasionally – but if what you want is a numbered list of action points then buy a self-help book, don't see a therapist. Going back to Leslie Kenton's image of the sculptor and his block of marble, psychotherapy can be seen as much the same sort of process – only we are the sculptors of ourselves, the artists of our own personalities.

The day we are born – and many psychologists now believe the process actually begins earlier, in the womb itself – we start to be shaped by the people and events around us. It is no exaggeration to say that we are the adults we become because of the tone of our mother's voice as we lie in our cots, because of the atmosphere our parents and family create in the home as we toddle around with our toys, because of the love and affection we do or don't get when we need it. Everyone travels with luggage: and the baggage we collect as we journey through our lives can help or hinder us. Sometimes our baggage is useful, practical, necessary; sometimes it just gets in the way. We've all had the experience of arriving somewhere and realising with dismay that we have been lugging around a heavy suitcase full of entirely the wrong clothes – thick woollen sweaters for a tropical beach.

To conclude the analogy, that's where psychotherapy can help. It's about rationalising your baggage, dumping things that are no longer useful to you and sending them to the emotional equivalent of the Oxfam shop.

Psychotherapy is not a compulsory part of exploring your inner self, and the world is full of balanced happy people who get on just fine without it. Nor do you have to be driven into it by some precipitating crisis or breakdown – though it can be of enormous positive help. Many would say that spending some time talking with a trained professional who provides the safe space in which to discover yourself is just as healthy and normal an activity as, for instance, joining a gym because you want to shed some flab.

If you decide to see a psychotherapist, the organisation listed below will put you in touch with qualified practitioners. Personal recommendation is, as always, invaluable. Libraries, health-food or 'alternative' shops and health centres may also display the business cards of practitioners or leaflets about their work.

Short courses: It's also worth pointing out that all over the country there are now centres offering a variety of psychotherapeutic and complementary therapies. Typically, every such centre will offer classes and sessions in such things as yoga, the Alexander Technique, reiki, shiatsu and so on. Many of them also provide a base for counsellors and psychotherapists who may see clients individually, but also offer short introductory courses (lasting a day, a weekend or a couple of evenings) on subjects such as Transactional Analysis or Inner Child therapy. To find out about such centres close to you, look in *Yellow Pages* or *Thomson's* under Therapists.

The following are brief notes on a few of the various schools of psychotherapy. There are more, and this is the skimpiest of introductions.

Further Reading
Understanding Ourselves: The Uses of Therapy,
Joan Woodward, Macmillan.

For further information on counselling contact:
The British Association for Counselling
1 Regent Placc
Rugby
Warwickshire CV21 2PJ
Tel: 01788 578328
E-mail: bac@BAC.co.uk

Client-centred counselling

The person- (or client-) centred approach may also be called a humanistic approach to counselling, and some of the founding fathers of this movement include Gerard Egan, Eugene Heimler and Viktor Frankl. The main name you will hear, though, is the American Carl Rogers (1902–1987) who wrote many books about his approach to counselling in which he emphasises that three core conditions must be present in the therapist: empathy, genuineness and non-possessive warmth.

In client-centred counselling, no advice is given: the therapist is non-directional. You will never hear your therapist say 'you should' or 'you ought'. The therapist will avoid directly expressing his or her opinion – what he will do instead is reflect back to you his impressions of what you are feeling. For instance, the therapist may listen to you talking about an issue that concerns you greatly and comment 'I can sense that this causes you a lot of pain'.

Carl Rogers believed that each person already has the resources within to heal his or her own self. The client knows what is best: she may have lost touch with her own inner voice and feel unable to trust her own instincts, but the trust at the heart of client-centred therapy is that by purposeful talking with a counsellor, the client can recover the ability to listen to herself and direct her own life. The counsellor is a facilitator: his or her own personality should not intrude.

In client-centred counselling, you will find the word 'problems' replaced by the word 'issues'. This is significant, and especially perhaps for clients who seek help with stress-related issues. The reason is that the word problems may carry connotations of blame, and ultimately of resolution of the problem as a final solution. In other words, if A is my problem, and I can find a solution for A, then there will be no more problems. In fact, the 'problem' may re-occur in a different form because it is the result of an attitude or an unexpressed need on the part of the client; issues are the fabric of life. (As Freud would have said, unless a repressed emotion is named, it will continue to affect our lives in a variety of ways.) Problems do not have to necessarily be solved but lived with, understood, accommodated.

Eugene Heimler (1922–1991) used the experience of his own terrible suffering in Auschwitz to develop what he termed 'connective counselling'. In a wonderful phrase, he referred to the 'the pearl inside each of us' and felt that all life was a search to find meaning. In Auschwitz, he observed that some people gave up the struggle to live and died because they had lost all sense of meaning. In the search for meaning, Heimler said that we should connect our past with our present – present events have their roots in our past and only by integrating the two can we find wholeness.

A technique of value here is called the 'Slice of life'. The client thinks of a situation in the last 24 hours which has triggered pain or strong emotion (such as feelings of anger or jealousy). She is then invited to link the feeling engendered by that emotion with an event or happening in the deep past – usually in early childhood.

Gestalt therapy

The founder of gestalt, Fritz Perls (1893–1970)
trained in Freudian psychoanalysis but later
described psycho-analysis as 'crap'. Born in a
Jewish ghetto in Berlin, he left Germany with
the rise of Nazism and went to live in South
Africa, leaving only when apartheid was
introduced. He died in California.

The word gestalt itself is a German word
meaning 'whole' or 'pattern' or 'configuration',
and so the gestalt process is a holistic process –
that is, the mind, body and senses are all seen as
part of the same unity, not as separate elements.
Gestalt is described as an 'actualising' approach.
That means, the aim is to become who you are.
Perls felt that the individual beings we were
born to be become clouded and muddled by
struggling in society to be what others want us
to be. He wrote: *'A rose is not intent to actualise
itself as a kangaroo...In nature, except for the
human being, constitution, and healthiness,
potential, growth, is all one unified
something...We [humans] find ourselves on the
one hand as individuals who want to actualise*

themselves; we find ourselves also embedded in a society, and this society makes demands on us different from the individual demands. So there is a basic clash'.

Gestalt seeks to resolve this clash. The aim of gestalt therapy may be simply defined as 'awareness'. Awareness itself is therapeutic; when the mind is cluttered with needs which are not met or feelings which are not accepted it is said to be blocked with 'unfinished business', and it is the aim of gestalt – through facilitating awareness – to 'unblock' the individual and finish the business.

How then does it work in practical terms?

Gestalt is a 'quick' form of therapy: clients are usually only asked to commit themselves to a short number of sessions (often as few as four or six) whereas other types of counselling may be open-ended, but usually with a minimum commitment of several months. Gestalt often takes place in group sessions, and certain ground rules (or 'adjustments') are laid down for the group which help the individual adjust to the idea of 'taking responsibility for my own self' (which is a key gestalt building block). These adjustments include:

● In therapy, the client is not to speak about someone but rather to them – even if that person is not present, you should speak directly to them. Thus if you are talking to the therapist about your mother, you should address your remarks as if your mother were sitting opposite you. The idea behind this is that it encourages openness and responsibility but that we should also direct remarks and behaviour where they belong. (See the two-chair process, below).

● Make statements not questions. In gestalt, clients are encouraged to say *'I think that...'*or *'I want to....'* rather than *'Do you think I should?'* or *'Would it be a good idea if I...?'* This means you are asserting yourself and speaking for your own needs rather than seeking the approval of other people.

● Say *'I'* not *'one'* or *'people'*. Gestalt encourages individual responsibility. Thus you can only really say *'I want to do this'* or *'I feel that this is right'*. Using expressions like *'one does not always want to do this'* or *'most people would think...'* dilutes your individuality.

● Change the passive to the active. For example, instead of saying *'My boss upset me by saying that'* you should say: *'I allowed myself to become upset by what my boss said to me'*. The change in emphasis is clear: I take responsibility for the way I feel. People do not make me do things, I choose to do them.

In gestalt therapy, the client is encouraged to set up a dialogue or a series of dialogues with other parts of his own personality. As we saw above, Perls felt that conflict arose from who we want to be and really are, and the person who others think we are or ought to be. A technique of gestalt is to encourage a dialogue between these two parts and this is sometimes done by asking the client to use two chairs. When he sits in one chair, he is (for example) the person he really wants to be; when he expresses the views of the 'other', he must move to the other chair. In this very graphic way, the client comes to a literal awareness of the parts that make up the whole.

This technique can also be used when, in therapy, we need to place feelings where they really belong.

In other words, if a client considers himself an 'angry' person whose anger tends to spill out generally into all areas of his life, but he can recognise that that anger actually comes from his relationship with his father, then in the two-chair scenario he can 'be' both his childhood self and his father, and conduct a dialogue with his father, directing his anger, fully and focusedly, where it has always belonged.

Further Reading

Frederick S Perls, *Gestalt Therapy*. Souvenir Press.

Gaie Houston, *The Red Book of Gestalt*. Rochester

Muriel Schiffman, *Gestalt Self Therapy*. Wingbow

Richard G Abell, *Own your own Life*. Bantam

Transactional analysis (TA)

TA is a school of psychotherapy which, as its name implies, seeks to analyse the transactions of our lives: in other words, we don't exist in isolation but as part of a network of relationships – with family, with a partner, with colleagues and of course with our own selves. If we understand the nature of these various transactions and the way we handle them, we have a better understanding of ourselves.

The foundation stone of TA is the ego-state theory of personality. This means, that at any time I may be expressing my personality from one of three ego-states within myself. Whichever ego state I am in will define how I behave.

These three states are:

> Parent
>
> Adult
>
> Child

For instance, in comforting a friend and trying to be supportive, I could be acting from my Parent ego state: nurturing and loving. If I have to make a financial decision, I am probably acting from the Adult ego state, which sifts information and evaluates it and reaches conclusions based on evidence. Among friends or with family at home, I might be acting from Child, which is usually defined as playful and spontaneous.

Note that all the terms used in TA have a very specific meaning within TA. To be in a 'Child ego state' does not (necessarily) mean that you are being childish or even childlike. This use of everyday terms but with a new, deeper meaning is often quite baffling to those unfamiliar with TA.

Each ego state has positive and negative attributes. Our inner Parent, for example, may be a Nurturing Parent ('there, there, it'll be all right') or a Controlling Parent ('don't do that'). Our inner Child may be a Free Child (inquisitive, impulsive, adventurous) or an Adapted Child (trained and restrained) – as real children often become when they have very controlling parents. Adult seeks to bring balance and harmony: Adult is the voice of reason. Adult is a filter: the Parent and Child ego states have their roots in the past, with how your real parents were and how you were as a real child, but Adult is in the here and now, and concerned with today's reality. So for example if my Adapted Child inner voice says to me 'This is scary, I'll fail, better not do that' my Adult can step in and respond with: 'There's no evidence that you'll fail. Given the situation and what I know of the conditions, I think this is a sensible course of action'.

We can move between these ego states all the time and they are utterly flexible – unless, that is, there is a blockage somewhere (see below). And they are all needed. Controlling Parent, for example, might seem like a repressive force; but in fact it's Controlling Parent who tells you not to touch bare wires, and to look carefully before crossing the road.

A TA therapist will spend some time outlining this theory and explaining the characteristics of the different ego states. The reason, quite simply, is that we can see where we're coming from. Although I might like to think I spend a lot of my time acting from Adult – calm, rational, sensible – my time in TA therapy taught me to see just how much of the time I spend in Adapted Child, trying to please, trying to 'be good'.

When one ego state is dominant most of the time, or when movement to another ego state is blocked for some reason, there is an imbalance. A healthy personality may be defined as one in which the individual moves happily between all five go states in an appropriate way, as the circumstances demand. In some personal relationships, for instance, one partner may spend most of the time acting from Controlling Parent and the other partner from Adapted Child. All is 'well' until Adapted Child wants to move into Adult, say – the transaction then becomes crossed or blocked. What TA therapy seeks to do is unblock our free access to the component parts of our personality and give us choice over which state to be in. It is a simple, straightforward and very direct way of understanding our personality and therefore our behaviour.

My outline is a gross simplification, however, and I do urge the interested reader to read a fuller account of what TA is and what it can do. Recommended books are listed below and they in turn contain fuller reading lists.

Many other ideas underpin this basic structure of TA and I only have room to mention a few very briefly here, because they have particular relevance to stress.

Strokes

We need to be 'stroked' -- literally. Recent studies in Romanian orphanages have shown that abandoned babies die from a lack of physical contact: their spines fail to develop, and their little bodies shrivel and perish. Babies cannot develop normally if deprived of the touch of hands and the warmth of a maternal, or proxy maternal, body.

Dogs and cats lick their puppies and kittens constantly: they are not just grooming them and bonding with them, they are actually stimulating appetite by licking and so helping their offspring to grow.

As babies, we needed the physical touch of our mothers but as adults we need strokes too: we need friends, family and colleagues to validate our worth. Here are some examples of things we might say which 'stroke' other people in a positive way.

- *I love you.*

- *Gosh, this is a great casserole.*

- *I could not have done this without you.*

- *These sales figures are just what I wanted.*

Saying 'thank you' as you get off a bus is stroking the driver: you are acknowledging his existence and validating him, that is, acknowledging that he is a separate and important individual.

Strokes can be negative, too, and we all have experience of these:

- *Why do you always have to wear that ghastly coat?*

- *What kind of sales figures do you call these, Smith?*

- *Is that the best you can do?*

- *I hate you.*

- *Leave me alone.*

- *Bloody kids, get off my garden.*

We can also reject positive strokes. If someone says *'you look wonderful'* and you respond with 'you need your eyes testing, my hair looks awful' this is a mild form of rejecting a positive stroke; the exchange *'I love you' 'No you don't'* is a very emphatic rejection of a stroke.

Discounting leads on from negative stroking, for discounting means ignoring or devaluing a person or an experience. The parent who neglects or ignores their child (even if only temporarily) is discounting them. The wife who says loudly in a restaurant: 'My husband won't have the Pavlova. He's got a weak stomach and rich puddings keep him up all night' is discounting: talking about a real, present being in the third person, depriving them of their own individuality and responsibility for themselves.

Scripts and games

TA says that individuals in whom the Adult is not developed, people who do not function as autonomous beings, follow a 'script' of life and play 'games', and a common tool in TA therapy is to encourage the client to examine their own life for traces of script and game-playing. (In most of us, it's unavoidable). Various fun devices (such as encouraging people to think of a slogan to put on a T-shirt which encapsulates their life position, or write their own epitaphs) have a serious goal: to help us spot repetitive patterns of behaviour (scripts).

Eric Berne, the founder of TA, identified numerous games in his book *Games People Play*. Many of us will have played at least one of them at some time or another. The point of a game is that it brings a pay-off to those who play it: both parties gain something (even if it's negative, usually because it's negative) and a game cannot be played if one party is aware that it is a game, and withdraws from it.

Let's take one extreme example to illustrate

this. A man is alcoholic. There will be a trigger point – a bad day at work, a nagging letter from the bank, his parking space taken by someone else – and he will go on a drinking spree. This leads to a row at home with his wife, whom he abuses verbally and physically. He is then overcome by remorse, breaks down, begs for forgiveness, promises to reform. His wife forgives him, and peace is restored. And then the whole game can begin all over again.

What is the pay-off here? On the surface, it appears such a distressing situation for all concerned. But this is the important point about games: they cause such havoc and unhappiness, but for the players, this is the only way to get in touch with their deepest reality.

It is a basic theory of TA that our deepest reality (the feelings with which we feel most comfortable and at home) may in fact be negative and unhappy emotions. This is because this is the earliest reality we lived with, as a child. As babies and children we don't know and can't use words; we only know feelings. And if the only feelings we know are bad ones, then, subconsciously, that's what we try to get back to.

In the story above, the man learned as a child to feel 'comfortable' with his own self-hatred: as an adult, abusing himself through drink followed by bad behaviour towards another person is a sure way of achieving regular 'fixes' of self-hatred. A great part of the game is his conviction that he is not responsible for his drinking: other people make him do it.

As for the woman, it's likely given the circumstances that she had a discounting father (that is, one who ignored her) and who created around her an atmosphere of instability and upset. In subsequent relationships, she may say that she's looking for a caring, loving man 'not at all like her father' but in fact she is only 'comfortable' (that is, she only feels quite literally 'at home') in an environment which exactly replicates the emotional chaos of her childhood.

In exploring our inner selves, the following TA issues may be helpful.

● Responsibility. Nobody makes you do or feel things, you permit yourself to feel or act in certain ways . This is not a 'fault' and indeed in the circumstances may be perfectly understandable – but accept your feelings as your responsibility, something that is yours, not other people's.

● If you are game playing, or among people who play games as a (probably subconscious) way of manipulating others, you will feel very stressed. If you can spot repetitive patters of negative behaviour in those around you – in which you are involved – which lead to a crisis and a pay-off before they start up all over again, then you have the chance of withdrawing yourself from such negative activity.

● If you feel that certain negative emotions or behavioural patterns are a regular part of your life, and come from 'unknown' places deep within yourself, then the script of your life – a script developed in your earliest childhood – can be changed.

● You are not the only one acting from one of the five ego states: so is everyone else.Thus when your boss gives you a negative stroke by saying *'Haven't you finished yet?'* and your automatic reaction is to feel *'I've failed'*, analysing the situation in TA terms and realising that you have gone straight into blame-taking Adapted Child (while the boss obviously wishes to be Controlling Parent) brings perspective and balance to a stressful situation and shows you how to resolve it – by choosing to move into Adult and handling it that way ('No, actually I didn't have enough time').

The key to changing any area of your life or your behaviour is first of all awareness. Awareness of what the patterns are, of what – in therapy speak – the issues are. Therapy can help to uncover your awareness and in so doing give you the support you need while change takes place.

Further Reading

Ian Stewart and Vann Joines, *TA Today*. Lifespace

Muriel James and Dorothy Jongeward, *Born to*

Win. Addison Wesley

Thomas A. Harris, *I'm OK, You're OK*. Arrow

Eric Berne, *Games People Play*. Penguin

Cognitive therapy

Cognitive behaviour therapy has its origins with the Russian scientist Pavlov and his experiments with dogs. A bell rings, food is brought to a group of dogs, the dogs see the food and begin to salivate in anticipation, and they are fed. Eventually, the dogs begin to salivate when the bell is rung – they know what to expect next.

This, Pavlov argued, is also applicable to humans: behaviour is learned from experience. At the heart of cognitive therapy lies the belief that what is learned can also be unlearned if it proves not to be helpful to us.

There's an old saying 'success breeds success' and recent studies among businessmen have shown that a positive outlook is linked with success. If you believe you will succeed, you and more likely to do so than the person with a negative outlook. Professor Jeffrey Gray of the Institute of Psychiatry analysed the acceptance speeches by American presidential candidates, and found that in 17 out of 20 elections, the candidate who won used the greater number of optimistic phrases.

'Optimism' in this context has a special meaning. Professor Gray says that there are three aspects to the explanations we give for what happens: these are internal, stable and pervasive.

Imagine this conversation, for instance. A man is late for a business meeting and his boss asks him why. 'My plane was delayed by fog', he replies calmly. To analyse this reply using the three aspects –

Internal	He is not blaming himself for being late; external circumstances were to blame and there was nothing he could do about it
Stable	The fog is not permanent; he won't be late next time and he wasn't late last time
Pervasive	Delayed by fog is one minor incident and it doesn't colour his whole career: he is not a less valuable or experienced worker because of this

The 'pessimist', on the other hand, would internalise and agonise over the whole situation, taking blame for the fog, the late arrival of the plane, his boss's anger, and everything else upon himself.

Cognitive therapy works in a limited number of sessions (usually no more than 15 and often about 10) to help people observe themselves being negative or pessimistic, and to change their behaviour. When clients are encouraged to be positive and optimistic, this does not mean they should be unrealistically so: it's simply that when the facts of the situation are observed, negative attitudes often don't 'stand up in court'.

Many forms of therapy begin with the past, and in delving into their childhoods clients may be overwhelmed by emotion. Cognitive therapy focuses more on thinking, and on the here and now.

Many therapists work by asking the clients to keep a series of charts describing real situations and the feelings they had or have about them which are then discussed during sessions. An example of such a chart might go like this:

Feeling: *I'm utterly depressed and wretched and useless. I don't want to go on.* Situation: My boyfriend has just dumped me and is going out with someone else.

Thought: *I hate myself, I'm worthless, if I was as good as his new girlfriend he wouldn't have dumped me, I'm not as good as she is.*

Alternative thought: *I am not worth nothing just because a relationship ends and leaves me in pain. I'm feeling pain because I'm a real, human person who can be hurt. My boyfriend's behaviour is his responsibility, I don't have to dwell on it and get bitter, I have my own life to get on with – a life that was whole before I met him and will be so again soon.*

Outcome: The client's negative thoughts had followed her ex-boyfriend out of the door; she had sent her own sense of selfhood after him instead of keeping it firmly focused upon herself.

Cognitive therapy is a useful tool for living, and can be of benefit to those who feel themselves at odds with their inner selves.

Dysfunctional people feel in themselves a conflict between the person they want to be, or think they really are, and the way in which they find themselves acting or thinking. This may be because negative behaviour patterns have been established in childhood; you want to be rid of these because they hold you back and prevent you being 'the real you'.

If the causes of the stress caused by such dysfunctional behaviour can be looked at individually in this manner, and optimistic responses put in place of more negative ones, the stress will resolve. For example:

Feeling: *I'm useless and worthless, I don't deserve to have a job, this whole situation's gone pear-shaped.*

Situation: I *lost that important contract with Bloggs and Bloggs.*

Thought: *I'll get the sack, I'll never get a job again*

Alternative thought: *Bloggs and Bloggs have been difficult customers for years and it's been obvious to all of us that our product is not quite right for them. We have other customers who are very happy with the service I give them, and my record is good. I've learned something from this experience, and I'm going to apply that when I deal with the new clients I'm going to go out and get.*

Outcome: *This person was taking responsibility that did not belong to him. He was seeing the defection of Bloggs and Bloggs as a personal failure, when the most likely reason is that there were a number of other commercial factors behind their decison.*

It's important to realise that cognitive therapy is not about letting individuals off the hook by saying 'it's not my fault'. If something is most definitely my 'fault', then I need to take responsibility for it, own up, and learn from the experience. But many of us feel that everything is our fault, and we enter a spiral of negativism when something goes wrong, believing that if one thing goes wrong, it's inevitable that everything else will. Experience shows that it does not.

Inner child therapy

'Getting in touch with my inner child' is a phrase often met with howls of derision by those who do not understand its meaning. It tends to be associated with the more extreme fringes of alternative therapies, on a par with concepts such as primal scream therapy or re-birthing (where clients work towards re-experiencing the actual moment of birth in order to dissolve the trauma they actually felt at that time). It is, however, a very important concept worthy of attention.

Inner child therapy will inevitably owe much to Transactional Analysis, and in fact many TA psychotherapists work in this way.

The child we all were – that small, emotionally fragile, vulnerable person, often confused or frightened by the oddities of the world, the punchbag for adult egos (often quite literally) – is still there, inside us. Physically we may be bigger and as we grow we develop techniques for handling the world and for hiding our own child-likeness. Only by getting in touch again with the child we used to be, remembering that vulnerability and fragility, can we find wholeness. Our childhood years mold us: in John Bradshaw's phrase, our childhood is 'the core material of our lives that shapes all else: the filter through which subsequent experience passes'.

Often the real child we have inside us is still scared, a rather reserved person who has lost the ability to play (if we ever had it) and laugh and be spontaneous and carefree, the way children ought to be. Through getting in touch with our inner child, we can set free or re-discover those qualities.

There is another aspect of getting in touch with our inner child, too, and one that is particularly helpful with adults who have low self-esteem, or are too unforgiving of themselves, driving themselves too hard. Children tend to arouse in us feelings of protectivity; we want children to be safe, and nurtured, and surrounded by warmth and affection. How often, though, do we extend those feelings to our own adult selves?

Therapists sometimes encourage the client to imagine that she holds herself, as a small girl, on her knee. (I'm deliberately using a female client as an example; see below.) Visualise yourself as a child: what you wore, how you looked, whether you were skinny or plump, wore glasses or had grazed knees. Imagine that that small version of you is now sitting on your lap, in need of comfort and cherishing, crying perhaps from a wounding experience, and it is in your power to give this. Stroke and pet that child; comfort her; tell her she is loved, and safe with you.

Such visualisation exercises are used to bring us in touch with the reality of ourselves as small children, and to foster a sense of tenderness and kindness for our own selves.

In the example above, I suggested the client was female but the exercise is obviously of value both to men and women. Because of the difference in the way men and women are traditionally brought up, I suggest that it is more difficult for women to feel kind and nurturing towards their inner selves. Small boys are cherished by their mothers and brought up to be cherished by other women – sisters, girlfriends, wives, daughters; nurtured in this way, it is not difficult for them to extend their nurturing to their inner child. In traditional households, girls are brought up to look after other people: to nurture, but not to be nurtured. I accept that this is a pattern of child-rearing that is changing, but in my experience women tend to be far less tender and loving towards themselves than men.

The Swiss child psychologist Piaget called children cognitive aliens: meaning, their thought processes are different from adults. They are 'absolutisers': that is, if you do not love me, then you must hate me. There are no shades of grey with children, and they lack the experience (what in TA parlance would be called the developed Adult) to distinguish between shades of meaning and filter them through the common sense of perceived fact. To give an example, if you say to a child: 'You're ugly', that child has no mechanism for saying to herself or himself: 'Now wait a minute, that's a very subjective viewpoint and plenty of people would not agree'. The child will simply absorb the information as a fact, and internalise: 'It's true. I'm ugly.'

Two concepts – words that have a special meaning in the context of inner child work – are of interest here. One is contamination. Ideas and misconceptions absorbed unconsciously in our childhood 'contaminate' our adult selves and lives, and during therapy these contaminating beliefs will be named, identified and therefore disengaged from their power over us. Examples of contaminating beliefs are, for example, *'If I have money, everything will be OK'*; *'I cannot live without [my partner]'*; *'My mother loves me, and so I have to please her'*. None of these statements is necessarily true, but if we believe versions of these, they have the power to contaminate other areas of our lives.

The other concept is of toxic shame. Many therapists, working with adults who experienced difficult childhoods, have observed how they seem to feel a sense of being 'defective' or of little worth; they behave and think as if at some stage in their lives a very low value has been placed upon them, and they have accepted that. Typical feelings are *'I don't deserve this'*, 'good things don't happen to me', 'it's bound to go wrong because it's me.'

Therapists work alongside their clients to uncover the origins of such negative feelings, and reverse them.

Inner child therapy is often used in adults who have experienced the worst kinds of abuse as children. It is observed that adults who were sexually abused as children grow up with debilitating levels of toxic shame, of feeling themselves to be worthless. Many therapists emphasise however that there are different types of abuse, but they all, to a lesser or greater extent, have the same effect. While it would be wrong to donwplay the suffering of a child who is sexually or physically abused, parents for – for example – routinely shout at their children, or criticise them, are offering a form of abuse which has devastating effects in adult life.

Further Reading

Alice Miller, *The Drama of Being a Child.* Virago

John Bradshaw, *Homecoming.* Piatkus

John Bradshaw, *Healing the Shame that Binds you.* Health Communications

Counselling for a specific event

The terms psychotherapy and counselling are often used interchangeably. A useful distinction that has been made between the two is that whereas psychotherapy seeks to help the client understand his or her life as a whole, individuals tend to seek counselling for help with a specific crisis. Bereavement counselling and post-traumatic stress counselling are two examples of this; the individual needs support in coping with one particular devastating incident.

In practice, however, the distinction is not that clear-cut and there is considerable (and probably desirable) overlap.

A traumatic event such as bereavement can often catapult people into a need for greater self-awareness as they struggle to work through the bereavement process and come to terms with their new situation. The skills needed by counsellors – those of active empathetic listening, and a respect for the integrity of the client – are precisely those of the psychotherapist.

Counselling has recently come under fire for ineffectiveness and it is fashionable to sneer at the haste with which organisations rush to announce that they are making counselling available after some traumatic incident. While there is such a thing as bad and ineffective counselling, it's also necessary to have a clear idea of its aims and much of this bad press arises through a lack of understanding of what counselling is for. Too many people mistakenly look for the quick fix. There is none. Grieving or recovery from trauma is a long, painful process, with many distinct stages to be gone through. Counselling offers support and an understanding of the process: nothing, alas, can take away the pain.

Time out

Most religions have a tradition whereby, when a person is seeking some truth about themselves or about the world, they withdraw from it for a while. Before Jesus Christ began his ministry, we are told he went into the desert for forty days and nights; in Biblical terms, he went there to fast and pray, but we might say he'd gone away to 'think about things' or 'find himself'.

In the Buddhist tradition, the pampered prince, Gautama Siddhartha (the Buddha) left his luxurious life at court and spent six years wandering as a penniless ascetic. While sitting beneath a banyan tree at the end of this self-imposed period of retreat, enlightenment came to him.

In our own day, when people say they want to find themselves, they often do so in quite extreme ways. During the 60s and 70s, many privileged middle-class young people took to the road with a backpack, exploring the so-called hippie trail to India. This often rather missed the point of self-exploration, which demands a degree of loneliness, self-reliance and pure and simple hardship.

The solicitor-who-jacks-it-all-in-to-become -a-crofter has also become something of a cliché in recent years, although it would be a mistake to criticise such a person too readily; making a radical change in lifestyle (and financial expectations) is not undertaken lightly. The fact is that the generations of the 30s, 40s and 50s worked because they had to, because jobs were scarce and there was no social security fabric to support them. A war intervened, and lives focused on survival. People whose children were born during or after that war quite naturally wanted for them the things they had not enjoyed: uninterrupted free education, a choice of lucrative employment, financial stability for life.

What a shock it was to those parents later on when many of those educated for white-collar middle-class 'safe' jobs, or the even safer professions, were either made redundant during the massive downsizing operations of the 80s and 90s, or decided, of their own free will, that they had had enough the rat race and the backstabbing, phony atmosphere of corporate politics, and went off to do something else. From television's The Good Life onwards, such people have inspired admiration, riducule – and not a little envy.

In the 90s, New Age travellers and eco-warriors attracted attention as the spiritual heirs of the hippies of 1960s. Their outright rejection of the plastic, rule-bound, apparently stifling world of suburbia or the British middle classes is courageous to some, repellent to others; but all would surely agree they have chosen a dramatic alternative to the way most people live.

It's possible that as you re-assess your life, a dramatic change comes to seem inevitable. For most people, this comes as a result of a long-buried ambition or desire. Take the case of Jackie, for instance, who had wanted to be 'something like a physiotherapist' when young but, for a variety of reasons (including the length of training, which to her at 17 seemed endless) took a better-paid job in marketing. Fifteen years on Jackie is single, 32, and steadily climbing the corporate ladder. But she comes, more and more, to regret that she is not doing something worthwhile in her eyes and through a chance meeting decides she wants to become an osteopath. Because she is single-minded and hardworking, she was able to complete 18 months of her osteopathy course part-time, studying at weekends and in the evenings. Before this she'd been a well-paid executive, but in order to finance her course she sold her car and gave up foreign holidays and ski-ing, a sport she loved. Finally the demand of her studies grew too great and she gave up her marketing job, re-mortgaged her flat, took out a bank loan and carried on studying. Although the days of designer clothes and holidays in Bali are (for the moment at least) a thing of the past, she has no regrets whatsoever and feels she is truly pleasing herself for the first time in her life, and doing something meaningful.

Redundancy can be turned from a disaster into an opportunity. Rob left school at eighteen and took a degree in accountancy. His father had been a low-grade civil servant and impressed upon Rob the importance of a well-paid job with prospects. Rob duly qualified and went to work, although his heart was never in it and he worked for a multi-national company in which office politics played a large and uncomfortable part. But Rob had married, and he and his wife Carol chose to have three children and decided that Carol would stay at home to look after them. It seemed the right decision for the family, but as the years passed the work pressures on Rob became greater and his health suffered. He started to suffer from asthma and a bad back, and found himself drinking too much whisky in the evenings. One Christmas the company was taken over by another, and Rob was made redundant. As they had a large mortgage and Carol was only qualified as a secretary, it seemed a disaster.

With Carol's support, though, Rob took the plunge and changed his life. His redundancy package meant he had enough money to keep the family going for a year and retrain as a primary school teacher, something he had always wanted to do. It was a struggle for a while, but once he'd qualified he found a job in a country school in Cumbria and he and Carol were able to exchange their executive home in Reading for a stone house in the Pennines and run a bed-and-breakfast business to supplement his teaching income.

These two examples have something in common, namely that the people were able to make a dramatic change in their lives because their previous lifestyle supported that change to some extent. Others are not so lucky, and may feel trapped in low-paid jobs they dislike, unable to make that break because of a lack of funds or because of their financial obligations to other people.

But if you sincerely believe that you need to change your life – that there is some other job you would rather do, some other life you would rather lead – then it is worth exploring every possible option in order to achieve that goal. There can be few things more regrettable than a life of 'I wish I had…but I didn't'.

A useful technique that has been recommended for thinking about life changes is a form of visualisation. Sit down alone with a piece of paper and write a description of how you want your life to be different. Imagine that you can make it happen, and start by writing 'A year from now, I could be…'

This is a serious exercise, and so you should of course discount at once things which belong in the realm of fantasy, such as winning the lottery. This is you being utterly honest and writing what you really, really want to be doing one year from now, or on your way to doing. You do not have to show this to anyone – particularly if what you'd rather be doing does not involve your family, or would cause them anxiety.

Work through the practicalities of what you want. If, for instance, you want to live in the country, then make practical notes: how much is your present house worth? Which area would you choose? How would you and your partner get to work, or could you work from home? Does this mean you'd have to change jobs, too? What about schools, shops, the price of petrol?

If you really really want to change your job – study for a new career, for instance – then where would you train? How would you travel there, or is it residential? How could this be financed? Have you got the necessary qualifications and application forms?

Two points emerge from such an exercise, if

carried out properly. The first is that if this is just a pipedream – and we all have those, and there is nothing at all wrong with them – then you will pretty soon realise that this is so. You will come to see that actually you like where you live very much, it's just nice to have a fantasy of a country cottage without the reality of it (no public transport,damp, high maintenance costs, distance from nearest sports facilities, etc.) and you will continue to indulge that fantasy secure in the knowledge that that is what it is.

The second is that if you sincerely want to carry out this plan, then the next stage is to look for practical ways and means of doing so. These nearly always exist if we search hard enough. If the price of changing your life in the way you think you want is giving up holidays for a couple of years, and travelling by bus so that you can sell your car, but you don't want to do this – then I suggest you don't really want to make this dramatic change after all.

And there's nothing wrong with that, either.

Retreats

Going into some form of retreat, religious or otherwise, is a good way of getting some personal time out to reflect on changes you may want to make in your life, or just to get a new perspective on the life you have.

A retreat can last as long as you like and have the money and time for, but is seldom of value if it lasts less than two or three days. A long weekend is all that many people have time for. The essential point is that you put yourself out of reach of the phone, the television, radio and newspapers. Leave your mobile at home. Of course you will tell those who need to know where you are going so that you can be contacted in emergencies, but try to keep contact with the outside world to a minimum.

It's also important that you go on retreat alone. You won't be alone when you get there and new friendships are often struck on retreat. But try to keep your interaction with other people to a minimum, too: this isn't a social event, it's a time for you to have the space to withdraw inside yourself. Some formally-run retreats have rules about conversation, asking those on retreat to talk to others only at mealtimes or in the evenings. This is so that the rest of this valuable time is yours for meditation and thought.

'Retreat' is a rather austere word suggesting a religious seclusion from the world, which is of course what they originally were (and still can be). Some people may wish to go on such a structured retreat, and the best contact to be made should be through your local church. It's not necessary to be a practising Christian or even a regular church-goer to go on a religious retreat: in most cases the organisers are offering a time out from the world to anyone who wants to spend private time in thought and contemplation. You will, however, not surprisingly find a Christian focus to such retreats and some are definitely only for practising Christians.

There are plenty of alternatives, though. All over the country there are secular places, usually formed around a permanent community such as the Findhorn community in Scotland, where outsiders are welcome to come and stay for a few days. In Dumfries-shire, there is the Samye-Ling centre at Eskdalemuir. This is a Buddhist temple where a community of monks and nuns live and work, but a limited number of visitors are also welcome on a paying basis. Occasionally there are short courses run by outsiders on subjects such as the Alexander Technique; students come for a weekend of learning about the technique, but in the peaceful and remote surroundings of the community.

Some people who plan to give themselves a few days of 'me time' will want to spend that time at a health spa. This is a wonderful treat for the stressed and the exhausted: a few days of being physically pampered in a luxurious environment oriented towards health, fitness and wellbeing. Although in most cases there is no spiritual element to such places, there is no reason at all why you cannot take your own spiritual focus with you. Whereas most people may spend the time in between treatments or exercises lying on their beds reading a book, you can take along some relaxation tapes and spend the time in meditation, or in writing a diary of your thoughts and feelings.

Another good idea (and less expensive) is simply to go away by yourself for a few days and spend the time camping or staying in a bed-and-breakfast. Try to go somewhere like Scotland, Wales, the Lake District or Dartmoor, and plan to spend every day walking. Alone in the fresh air, tramping over hills, moors and dales, you will find your mind clearing and focusing and giving you really valuable time to un-knot your thoughts. Such a break needs a certain amount of structure, of course: you will have to plan your walks, though there are now a number of books which do this for you. You will need safe and proper equipment and be prepared for sudden changes in the weather, even in the height of summer. Being free and alone on a Scottish hillside can sound wonderfully romantic and indeed it is; but be sensible too. Always tell someone where you are going and be properly equipped. And ignore my earlier comment about leaving your mobile phone at home if you're going to be miles from anywhere – while you should not spend your time maintaining your social life, any remote and uninhabited corner of the country is exactly the short of place in which you should have one.

The Samye Ling Centre may be contacted at:
The Samye Ling Centre
Eskdalemuir
Dumfries-shire DG13 0QL
Tel: 013873 73232

A company called CAER specialise in Cornish retreats at:
CAER
Rosemerryn, Lamorna
Penzane
Cornwall TR19 6BN
Tel: 01736 810530

Self-help through books and groups

Since the late 1960s and the growth of Encounter groups in the USA, this has been the age of the self-help manual and the self-help group.

It may seem a contradiction in terms to embark on a journey of self-discovery by joining a group, but in fact the shared experience of individuals, all of whom are at various stages on the same journey, can be comforting and beneficial.

A majority of self-help groups exist to provide a meeting ground for people with a similar disorder or affliction; the earliest and best-known example being Alcoholics Anonymous, founded in the US in the 1930s. The Twelve-Step programme envolved by AA has been so successful in helping so many that it has been widely emulated by other groups for those with all kinds of addiction, for example, Narcotics Anonymous and Gamblers Anonymous.

The key to such groups is safety. Whether you are an alcoholic or a drug addict, or whether you suffer from some illness or disorder, you need to feel absolutely and entirely safe in sharing your story. Vulnerable people do not want to be patronised, or 'told what to do', or have that vulnerability exploited. The whole point about AA is that everyone in that room is an alcoholic: confidentiality and safety are assured.

When struggling with an addiction, the hardest part is explaining to another person (doctor, employer, partner) what it's like. To those whose gambling is confined to a lottery ticket or a fiver on the Grand National, the person who puts their job, their home and their financial security on the line because of gambling is hard to understand; to those who enjoy a glass of wine of an evening, the alcoholic who reaches for a drink in the morning to stop shaking is an alien being. Nobody can understand an addict except another addict, and in that understanding – and, by implication, acceptance – healing can begin.

The AA programme, as has been suggested, offers very specific advice for people trying to live without alcohol, advice aimed at developing self-esteem and a positive self-image. Alcoholics are advised not to say 'I'll never touch a drop again' – only to try, just for today, not to lift a drink. To make grand claims of renunciation is to invite disaster; all we can do is live for the moment, for the day, and just for today, they say in AA, and with help from a power higher than myself (which some call God, although AA is not a religious organisation and the higher power can be anything which you deem it to be), I will not pick up a drink

Most of my comments about self-help groups have been about groups of people struggling with addictions, but groups now exist for – to name but a few – people with AIDS, people with eating disorders, and people suffering from cancer. The underlying principles are the same: a group of people who share one thing in common come together not to condemn or to criticise but to share, to talk, to laugh and cry, and to understand each other in a way that no one else can.

The plethora of self-help books that has

been published in the last 20 years cannot, of course, come close to offering what a group of individuals can. Many are no more than checklists of good advice, easily forgotten. But they do have a role to play, and many people have found them a help in their search for understanding. If for no other reason, they teach you that you are not alone. If a book has been written about a particular 'problem' – personal relationships, for example, or compulsive eating, or poor self-esteem – then you may be sure there is a market for it; which means you're not the only one who thinks or behaves in a certain way.

At the risk of repetition, it may seem contradictory to say that our journey to self-discovery can only be done by ourselves alone, and in the same breath to suggest finding others who are doing the same – but it works. Other people are a mirror in which we can see ourselves; and we all have different destinations, but can enjoy the companionship of the journey.

Alcoholics Anonymous, 0345 697555

Drinkline (information and counselling services) 0345 320202

Further Reading

Carla Perez, *Getting off the merry-go-round.* Impact

Stephen Smith, *Addict.* Westworld

Beauchamp Colclough and Elton John, *The Effective Way to Stop Drinking* Penguin

Terence T. Gorski, *Understanding the Twelve Steps.* Simon & Schuster

Jan Sutton, *Healing the Hurt Within.* Pathways

Religion

The search for God – or at least, the search for an answer as to what, if anything, is beyond this present world – is an old as the life of human beings on this planet.

It is not the purpose of this book to suggest that church-going (or regular attendance at mosque or synagogue or temple) is a good way of finding yourself, but sooner or later as we learn more about ourselves, we wonder about things spiritual. Very few would deny the feeling that, apart from body and intellect, there is a spiritual instinct within them. 'I don't go to church', we hear many say, 'but I consider myself a religious person'.

The nation's churches may be largely empty on a Sunday, but it is interesting to observe how, in moments of deep national crisis or distress such as the death of Princess Diana or the Dunblane massacre, those same churches suddenly fill or people find themselves wanting to make gestures – the leaving of flowers, the lighting of candles – which can be said to have a religious symbolism to them. The world can seem, as we know, a cruel and senseless place; religion and the observation of religious practice can offer a sense of order, of comfort, of meaning.

I have referred earlier to the work of the psychotherapist Eugene Heimler, a survivor of Auschwitz. It was a basic principle of Heimler's work that human beings need to have meaning in their lives – more than money, or success, or sex, or fame, or love, we hunger for life to mean something.

The creative artist is driven by the meaning given to his or her life by their art: the music, the dance, the painting or the act of writing without which their life is purposeless. Many who have given birth, or fathered children, feel that this has similarly given some point and purpose to their existence.

The religious or spiritual person may well find that a belief in God, whether or not that extends to membership of an organised world religion, invests their life with meaning.

Karl Marx described religion as the opium of the people. By this he meant that just as the drug opium induces in its users a sleepy sense of euphoria and paralyses the will, religious practice dulled people into submission and a dumb acceptance of the injustices of the world. There is, of course, a great deal of truth in this and over the centuries religion has been used as a tool for the cynical manipulatation of the masses. If you believed that God had made you poor and ignorant, and that the King was ordained by God to govern the country, and that you would surely burn in hell forever if you disobeyed any of the commandments either of God himself or of his 'deputies' on earth, then there was a certain point in maintaining the status quo.

For hundreds of years, in many cultures, the will of God was inseparable from the political will of the ruling elite. In fundamentalist Islam today, that philosophy prevails, while many would argue that the President of the United States is not above playing 'the God card' when it suits his purpose.

But the world has changed, and the most dramatic changes have taken place in the past couple of hundred years. Religion has become a matter of choice for most people, rather than an obligation imposed from on high, and it has been the choice of many not to participate in organised religious practice.

Many would argue that this has gone hand-in-hand with the decline of what are often called 'family values'. And it is true that in the days when church attendance was virtually obligatory in Britain – and certainly in rural areas – then the church was a focal point of the community, bringing people together in a way that does not happen now. In addition, the Christian churches traditionally forbade divorce and condemned homosexuality, 'living in sin', pre-marital sex and other behaviours which we today largely take for granted. While few would genuinely want a return to the old days, it is easy to see why so many think fondly of a Golden Age when, they imagine, things were very different, and the confusion that is characteristic of so many people's lives and attitudes today was absent.

There was no Golden Age: in Victorian times, for instance, which some are so fond of holding up as an example of 'good values', London has the largest population of prostitutes of any city in the world, and many of them were children. Hypocrisy was rampant, and starchy Victorian pillars of the community were just as likely to be regular users of prostitutes as any of those men the News of the World would delight in exposing now.

The 'self' that we are seeking is made up of three components: mind, body, and spirit. In the later years of the twentieth century many of us are quite happy to develop our minds and there has been a tremendous resurgence of emphasis on the body. The importance of health and exercise are impressed upon us ad nauseam.

But we should not forget the third part, spirit, either. That people have a spiritual need – just as strong as the need for intellectual stimulation or physical wellbeing – is proved by the fascination shown in recent years for all sorts of unusual cults and sects. These range from paganism, druidism and Goddess Worship to well-known sects such as the Church of Scientology or the Jehovah's Witnesses. In the 60s, the influence of the hippie movement led to a rekindled interest in a variety of Eastern faiths, practices and philosophies. In the 90s, Buddhism became the designer religion of the trendy. (It is interesting that the Dalai Lama himself has remarked that he is not particularly interested in converting people to Buddhism as he feels that people are probably most comfortable, if they have religious leanings, in getting to know the religion of their own culture better).

Some of these other faiths and traditions have much to teach us, and even a brief acquaintance with them can enrich our lives. An example of this would be Buddhism, with its non-violent traditions and emphasis on compassion and living in the present.

Of those that come under the label 'sects', some are quirky, most are harmless, and a handful downright weird and dangerous, preying on vulnerable and lonely people, eager to part them from their money and often their sanity too.

Personality type

Why are people different, and in what ways? If it is true that individuals are unique, but that they also fall into broad-based categories according to a general type, then finding out what type of person we are can help in a definition of our own uniqueness.

The most important work in this area was started by the psychoanalyst Carl Gustav Jung (1875-1961), a contemporary and one-time colleague of Freud, whose name will crop up again in the the section on Dream interpretation. Jung once wrote 'my life has been permeated by one goal...to penetrate into the secret of the personality..All my work relates to this one theme'. It was by understanding the mysteries of the human heart that Jung felt people could find fulfilment and become the fully developed people we are all born to be.

Jung's theory was that we all have a preference for a certain 'ways of being', or personality type. The key word here is 'preference' because nothing about personality is fixed or unchanging. But we do have definite tendencies and Jung defined these as:

Extrovert *or*	Introvert	(How we relate to the outside world)
Sensing *or*	Intuitive	(How we gather and use information)
Thinking *or*	Judging	(How we make decisions)
Feeling *or*	Perceiving	(How we organise ourselves and the world)

In other words, when it comes to how we relate to the world around us, people can either be extrovert (outgoing, life-and-soul-of-the-party, taking charge, perhaps bossy) or introvert (inward looking, thoughtful, focused). All the terms used above have a special meaning within Jung's theory and are not dictionary definitions, and it's important to be clear that every preference has both positive and negative aspects.

With natural extroverts, their energy flows out into the world and their environment; with introverts, their energy is contained within themselves. The world needs both types, but extroverts and introverts tend to misunderstand each other and devalue the qualities of the other. If you are a get-up-and-go type who wants to solve everything this second and go out and take on the universe, you will be utterly frustrated by the thinker who wants to work everything out on paper first. Extroverts communicate with the world; introverts communicate first with themselves. 'Why do you never tell me anything?' is often the cry of the exasperated extrovert to the introvert. The introvert will communicate, but only when he has first worked out exactly what he wants to say, and this may take some time.

In work situations, conflict between introverts and extroverts is almost inevitable unless they can learn to value each other's strengths and have patience with their very different ways of working.

In being either an extrovert or an introvert, Jung described this as your 'attitude to the world'. The other four types relate to functions of personality, that is, how we operate. If in the make-up of your personality the Thinking or the Feeling tendencies are uppermost, then you tend to be a rational person who evaluates things in the light of experience: a hard facts person. If sensation or intuition are uppermost (the so-called feminine qualities), then you tend to trust your hunches and your perceptions.

We've all heard conversations in which one person yells 'but where's the evidence?' and the other person keeps saying 'I just have this feeling about it'. Both people in such an exchange are being absolutely true to their personality type, which approaches the same reality from the opposite direction.

You cannot change the basic preferences of your personality, but Jung was convinced that our 'external' persona carried its 'shadow' with it. In other words, we contain our opposite qualities within ourselves – sometimes, particularly in times of stress, this shadow can become uppermost and we apparently act 'against type'. When people who know us say things like 'I don't know what's got into you, this is not like you at all' then it's likely we are living in the shadow part of our personality.

According to Jung, the middle years of life are often a time when we enter the shadow – what we would now call the mid-life crisis. It's as if we have spent the hot and energetic years of youth living in one side of our characters, busily engaging with the world and making our way in it and then, in the desire to re-evaluate and understand ourselves better, explore the other.

This may explain why some people make such radical life changes in their middle years and change careers, partners or lifestyles.

Further Reading

Maggie Hyde and Michael McGuinness, *Jung for Beginners*. Icon

Carl Gustav Jung, *Memories, Dreams, Reflections*. Fontana

Frieda Fordham, *An Introduction to Jung's Psychology*. Pelican

The Myers-Briggs Type Indicator

Two admirers of Jung's work, Katharine Cook Briggs (1875-1968) and her daughter Isabel Briggs Myers (1897-1980) developed the Myers-Briggs Type Indicator.

This is a written personality test in the form of a series of questions, for which you select from a number of possible answers. It may be completed in about 40 minutes and, when 'marked', indicates your personality type according to the Jungian preferences (there are 8 listed above, so 16 personality types altogether are described). More than 3.5 million Indicators are administered annually worldwide and used by all kinds of institution, company and social group as tools in understanding the people who work for them and in helping them to understand themselves. Isabel Myers was prompted to develop the MBTI because of what she saw as the appalling waste of human potential during World War II, where human individuality was so utterly disregarded.

The MBTI is a sensitive tool, and needs to be interpreted by a qualified professional. It is not the kind of questionnaire you see in glossy magazines ('How ambitious are you?') and has no benefit unless delivered by someone who can fully explain all the various types and their implications for co-operation or conflict. It must also be explained and emphasised that there is nothing right or wrong about any personality type; people are just different, and the MBTI seeks to celebrate that difference in unfolding it.

But once we understand that preference and personality type are an essential part of us and who we are (and that the same is true of everyone else) then it does become easier to understand why some relationships at work or in our personal lives are so stressful, why some groups of colleagues work productively together and others don't, why some situations gel and others are a disaster.

To find out more about using the MBTI in your workplace or personal life, contact Oxford Psychologists Press Limited (tel: 01865 510203). They may also be able to tell you of individual therapists in your area who administer the test.

Further Reading

Isabel B. Myers with Peter Myers, *Gifts Differing: Understanding Personality Types*. Davies-Black Publishing

Allen L. Hammer, *Introduction to Type and Careers*. Oxford Psychologists Press

Type A and B personalities

A much cruder definition of personality was made by two American cardiologists, Friedmann and Rosenman. They noticed that many of the patients who came to them with heart attacks and other stress-related cardiovascular problems shared similar characteristics, and that these personal traits made it difficult for them to follow their doctors' advice – namely, to relax, to avoid stress, to calm down and make lifestyle changes that would hopefully avoid further cardiac emergencies.

Friedmann and Rosenman defined their 'typical' patients as Type A and reported that men (and it usually was men) with Type A characteristics were six times more likely to suffer heart attacks than Type B personalities.

Type A personalities	Type B personalities
Create their own stress from within themselves	Accept stress only when it comes from the world outside, for example in a life event such as bereavement
Are highly competitive – winning is everything	Enjoy playing the game – winning is a bonus
Are always rushed and panic about the time available to them	Are relaxed, and thus use their time well
Are usually assertive (at best) or aggressive (at worst)	Are easy-going – not afraid to assert themselves, but never aggressive
Speak quickly and often fall over their words, explaining themselves badly	Think before they speak in clear, measured tones
Are impatient – 'why can't this be done now?'	Have a realistic attitude towards deadlines
Find relaxation impossible: a beach holiday with no mobile phone is their idea of hell	Know that relaxing well is as important as working well
Are socially inept: they hate small talk or chit-chat	Interact well with other people on several levels
Plan badly – always in a rush to do things, they don't prepare well	Are organised and make fewer mistakes
Find fault in the world around them and are often eager to apportion blame	Accept the world as it is, and know that blame is a useless indulgence
Feel they are what they do and they can only earn respect by doing it better than anyone else	Don't feel they have to prove anything – they are secure in their own sense of self-worth
Are easily bored and have short attention spans	Take pleasure in the here and now, and the small things of life – good food, good company, walks in the country
Believe the more they acquire the happier they will be	Want to 'live' not 'have'

You'll have noticed by now that Type A really are made to look like the bad guys, whereas all of us will rush to insist that we are Type B, who would seem to be practically saints. Basil Fawlty was clearly a Type A personality par excellence.

We need to remind ourselves again that personality is not fixed and rigid and that human beings are complex, intricate creatures capable of being many different things all at once. What is probably true is that most of us have characteristics of both Type A and Type B within us, and are capable of being either of those types at any given time.

If you do recognise parts of yourself in the Type A list, then it's almost certain that your health, your relationships and your happiness would all benefit from emphasising or trying to develop the Type B side of you.

It's evident that Type A people make their own stress: there's a voice within them saying 'Do it faster – work harder – stay later – drive yourself – go on' and that voice is something they have allowed to control their lives.

Type B's inner voice says: 'I am working to the best of my ability within the constraints of time and experience. I am a worthwhile person and I owe it to myself to look after my health and my wellbeing, to relax, to have fun and to love my life'.

Type A personalities seem to hate to play – maybe as children they were never allowed to play in that unstructured, carefree way that is important if children are to grow with a sense of the world being a good place to be, in which fun is not only possible but allowed. Type B knows that play is important because we need to rediscover our sense of fun and pleasure in the everyday.

Whenever you feel that your Type A has the upper hand, tell that inner voice to be quiet for a moment and let the good common sense of Type B take over. There is no evidence that Type B does not get the job done just as well or as fast or as effectively as Type A: there is only evidence that Type A is dreaded by his colleagues and has the heart attack, while Type B is having a good time somewhere else.

Further Reading
Patricia Hodges, *Understanding your Personality.* Sheldon Press

Paul Hauck, *Calm Down*. Sheldon Press

CHAPTER 3
THE PSYCHIC PLANE

At some point in their search for knowledge of themselves, many turn to more psychic approaches to self-discovery such as palmistry or clairvoyance. In many alternative bookshops or health-food shops throughout Britain, or in the classified ads section of a local paper, you will find advertisements for practitioners who claim, by a variety of means, to be able to give you an insight into your character and future.

Such claims are treated with scepticism by many, and it is as well to approach every such encounter with a healthy dose of detachment. For one thing, it is common for people to seek out clairvoyants when they are personally at a very low ebb – seeking an answer for an unhappy relationship, perhaps, or hoping to hear of an end to financial worries. Such distress or anxiety may make you vulnerable to charlatans and also makes you eager to believe anything you hear and interpret it without using your critical faculties.

Bear in mind also that clairvoyance is a bit like detective work. If you are a sensitive and observant person and have spent many years closely observing others, then some of the so-called insights put forward by clairvoyants seem obvious. 'She knew I was unhappy' is not quite so startlingly acute if, for example, the clairvoyant has noticed that her client has neglected to remove old nail polish, her clothes are too tight and her hair badly needs cutting. It's not unusual for women in distress to put on weight and neglect their appearance. The word clairvoyance means knowledge gained through extrasensory perception or 'second sight'; Sherlock Holmes was able to make quite startling deductions about his clients, too, using only the information of his own eyes and intelligence.

That said, the practice has been around for centuries and many people have made contact with gifted and sensitive clairvoyants whose insights have seemed uncannily accurate, and come away feeling reassured and all the better for it. There are too many recorded events of future events being foretold by psychics for clairvoyance to be dismissed out of hand.

Bear in mind, of course, that if a fortune-teller truly does see something awful in your future, she is highly unlikely – being a compassionate individual – to tell you in so many words! To give a crude example, no one is going to say: 'You will fall under a 39 bus a week on Tuesday' (always assuming that she has such accurate information) but rather: 'I'm sensing that you are unhappy and confused at the moment. Make sure you take special care of yourself when outside or in traffic, and concentrate on your own safety'.

As always, try to get a personal recommendation before you consult anyone.

Clairvoyants or fortune-tellers work in a number of ways. Strictly speaking, clairvoyance are psychics and may not normally 'tell the future'. Rather, they work by sharing the insights they gain from you in order to help you in understanding the issues in your life. They pick up information about the world about them in a heightened way. To give an example, someone who consults a clairvoyant because their son or daughter has left home and lost touch (always assuming this is not a police matter, and that they have left of their own free will) does so in the hope that the clairvoyant should suggest where they start their search. People often consult clairvoyants to find lost objects; it is also well known that the police sometimes use clairvoyants for help in locating dead bodies.

Fortune-tellers may work with tea leaves, with playing cards (this is called cartomancy) or with Tarot cards. Each card, or combination of cards, is said to denote something specific. In the normal pack of playing cards, for instance, the nine of spades represents misfortune and conflict; the eight of diamonds a late marriage or a happy journey; the king of clubs is a good, honest man; while the ten of hearts symbolises ambitions realised.

The Tarot cards, with their colourful and somewhat sinister representations (the hanged man, the devil, the tower, the judgement, the world) appear altogether more arcane and mysterious. Many claim a mystical aspect to the Tarot, and it has traditionally been linked with the practice of magic or the black arts.

Palmistry

Perhaps one of the most traditional methods of fortune-telling has been by palm-reading. Palmistry (or cheiromancy, as it is properly called, from the Greek word for the hand) claims to be able to reveal the true personality of the client, as well as foretell the future.

Serious palmists are, however, keen to point out that they do not predict the future so much as indicate tendencies or possibilities. This echoes what astrologers want to stress about free will, and the example given above of the woman who may or may not have an accident. Palmists prefer not to say 'this will happen' but rather 'there is a possibility this may happen, so be careful'. This is very much in line with other psychics who believe that personality type predicts tendencies. For instance, a high-octane, driven, stress-prone personality (and this may not be always apparent from their behaviour; some highly stressed people can appear quite calm) may well be more accident prone, or likely to have a heart attack if they don't pay particular attention to their health.

To say this is not to decry the skill of a palmist or any other competent and experienced practitioner, rather to emphasise that a truly sensitive and aware person may indeed pick up on tendencies not apparent to others.

The palmist makes a close study of the hand – its size, shape and general appearance – as well as looking at the raised areas of the palm, known as the mounts (the Mount of Jupiter, for instance, or the Mount of Venus). Just as a reflexologist claims to gain insights into a person's overall physical health through a study of the feet, so the palmist gains similar insights through the hand – by no means a far-fetched claim when you consider that our hands are our most basic tools, and that a number of medical conditions reveal themselves through the condition of the nails or the skin on the hands.

Further Reading
Peter West, *The Complete Illustrated Guide to Palmistry*. Element
Peter West, *Life Lines*. Foulsham

Astrology

In seeking to understand personality type, or find answers for the question 'Who am I?' many people have turned to astrology. In addition to defining and describing personality type, astrology also offers its adherents a glimpse of the future.

Astrology can arouse strong feelings in many people: there are those who deride it as poppycock and those who take it very seriously indeed. It is easy to see why it has become the subject of derision for many – for years now, in the UK, astrology has been no more than the reading of your horoscope in the daily paper; a fun thing to do, but absolutely not to be taken seriously. There are exceptions to this, of course, Jonathan Cainer being one example. His astrological advice tends to be general and philosophical, opting for the broader picture and not the discredited 'You will meet a tall dark man but don't let him any money. Wear the colour pink' approach.

Astrology too has been around for centuries, and when taken seriously is a very

complex art (the psychoanalyst Carl Gustav
Jung, who was interested in personality type,
was intrigued by the symbols and study of
astrology). Many famous people have taken it
very seriously indeed throughout history, and
in our own age former President Ronald
Reagan of the United States regularly consulted
astrologers before taking major decisions. In
the weeks before she died, Diana Princess of
Wales visited an astrologer in the company of
her friend Dodi Fayed.

As most people know, there are twelve signs
of the Zodiac – Aries the ram, Taurus the bull,
Gemini which is represented by twins, Cancer
the crab, Leo the lion, Virgo the virgin, Libra,
the sign of the scales, Scorpio the scorpion,
Sagittarius the archer, Capricorn the goat,
Aquarius the water-bearer and Pisces the fish.
These signs confer certain tendencies and
characteristics on those people who are born
under the sign, and in understanding the
characteristics of your sign, it is said, you can
reach a truer understanding of yourself.

In addition, each sign has certain affinities
and antipathies; each one is especially

associated with particular colours, gems, metals, countries and flowers. Many people find it helpful to surround themselves with the colours and objects with which their sign has an affinity although, oddly enough, they usually like them anyway!

There are many popular books describing the personality type of each sign, giving quite detailed descriptions of the attributes, preferred lifestyles, suitable professions, best romantic partners, likely health problems, ideal holiday destinations and so on for each one. A number of people are familiar with the basics of these, knowing, for example, that if you are a Sagittarian your 'best' choice of a mate should be either Aries or Leo, that likely professions to follow include journalism or the law, that Sagittarians have an affinity with Spain and Hungary and may suffer more from nervous disorders than any other type of health problem.

Many have found identification with their sign of the Zodiac helpful. Knowing the good and bad tendencies of being an Aries or a Capricorn can help people to accentuate the good and deal with the less good, while at the same time not being too hard on themselves for the negative attributes – *'Cancers are like that'*, *'I'm Leo, they always are too headstrong for their own good'* or *'Scorpios are difficult to get on with anyway'*.

As with anything, a belief in astrology can be taken too literally, or misinterpreted. Astrologers always point out that our good and bad points are listed not because they are immutable and fixed, but because there is freedom of choice and we have that in order to develop our good side and play down the bad. Not everyone born on 20 April turns into a Hitler, after all. Individuals are far more complex than any mere system of categorisation can account for, and we can all exercise choice in matters of behaviour and preference.

Astrologers are at pains to point out, however, that astrology is a complex art and in order to arrive at a true understanding of yourself you should consult a professional and have your own personal astrology chart compiled. For this they need to know the exact time and place of your birth in order to plot the positions of the sun and the moon at that time. These are variables which can make all the difference; if, for instance, you read a description of a typical Taurean and think 'I'm not in the least like that' the explanation, according to astrology, is because of the relative positions of the sun and moon at the exact time of your birth.

Further Reading

Sue Tompkins, *Aspects in Astrology*. (Element)

Carole Golder, *Astrology*. (Piatkus)

Warren Kenton, *Astrology*. (Thames and Hudson)

Peter West, *Astrology and Childhood*. (London House)

Dylan Warren-Davies, *Astrology and Health*. (Headway)

CHAPTER 4
DEVELOPING YOUR INNER RESOURCES

This chapter explores a variety of techniques, avenues and options that may be useful for the person exploring his or her inner self.

A common contemporary problem is the lack of time. We are all too busy, and yet there do not seem to be enough hours in the day to accomplish even half the things we need to do. The pressures of the workplace, or of juggling home and family lives, can all add to a sense of stress. This stress detracts from the sense of calm and balance we need if we're to cope meaningfully with life in the 21st century.

But it is one of those odd contradictions that the more time you make for yourself, to really relax and unwind, the more effective you can be when you return to the hurly-burly.

There are a whole host of techniques for relaxation – meditation, aromatherapy, reflexology, Shiatsu massage, Alexander technique – and many books available on each of those subjects. There is room here only to mention a few.

It is worth pointing out at this juncture that there are no statutory training requirements for most of the complementary therapies, though that will undoubtedly change as they grow in popularity and become more widespread. Almost anybody can – and some do – put a plaque on their door and announce they are this or that type of therapist or pracititoner. While the majority have studied for whatever qualifications are available in their field, and practice in good faith for the benefit of their clients, it is as well to be wary and to trust your instincts. As with anything else in life, personal recommendation is invaluable.

Many have reported the experience of taking up one or more of these complementary therapies and finding whole new aspects of their personality they did not know existed. 'I just felt I was a wholly different woman', a busy marketing executive reported when she started studying the Alexander technique. It was not the technique itself which changed her; once she relaxed, felt better about herself, and made more time to look within herself, she liberated aspects of her personality that had been repressed by the frantic pace she normally expected of herself.

Yoga

The word yoga means 'union' in Sanskrit, and refers to the union of body and soul which are the aims of the practitioner. In focusing the mind and stretching and relaxing the body, yoga instils a sense of wholeness and peace. The art itself is thousands of years old and has a variety of forms; while there are many books on the subject, the best way to get acquainted with yoga is to find a good teacher and attend classes.

Some make yoga a lifelong study, and are drawn to its spiritual side. Others simply find it a wonderful method of relaxing and becoming supple. In yoga there is an emphasis on correct breathing – which is of course crucial to relaxation – and on paying attention to the body, not forcing it or hurting it in any way, but gradually and gently building stamina and suppleness through a series of purposeful movements.

Yoga encourages self-consciousness in the best sense of the word: an awareness of your body and its movements, awareness of how you move and sit and react. This developing self-awareness can extend to behaviour also, and to the way in which your inner self presents itself.

Yoga positions seem very simple: indeed, if your acquaintance with yoga is limited to illustrations in a book, you may wonder what all the fuss is about. In many of them, the student sits or stands in one position, and 'merely' stretches. The actual experience of truly stretching the body, extending it, while being conscious of deep and rhythmic breathing, is like nothing else. The mind experiences stillness and refreshment. It is perhaps significant that many of the most common yoga positions taught in classes – the Cat, the Cobra, the Fish, the Dog – are named after other living creatures. In the animal kingdom, beasts can only express themselves through their bodies. A cat, for example, seems characterised from its physical qualities: graceful, effortless movements, an overwhelming appearance of relaxation. In the truest sense, animals live in and through their bodies in a way humans do not. If a cat or dog becomes overweight or sluggish it is the owner's fault for overfeeding and restricting exercise; in a more natural state, animals restrict their own appetite and balance it with the exercise they need. Dogs love to run and play; cats, less active but no less fit, stretch themselves to keep supple.

A study of yoga aims to impart that same sense of 'being comfortable inside your own skin' that we can observe in animals.

Further Reading

Dr R Monro, *Dr Nagarathna and Dr Nagendra*, Yoga for Common Ailments. Gaia

James Hewitt, *The Complete Yoga Book*. Rider

B K S Iyengar, *Illustrated Light on Yoga*. Thorsons

Swami Shivapremananda, *Yoga for Stress* Relief. Gaia

For more information on yoga and classes in your area, contact:

The Yoga Therapy Centre
Royal London Homeopathic Hospital
60 Great Ormond Street
London WC1N 3HR
Tel: 0171 419 7195

Scottish Yoga Teachers Association
Frances Corr
26 Buckingham Terrace
Edinburgh EH4 3AE
Tel: 0131 343 3553.

The British Wheel of Yoga
1 Hamilton Place, Boston Road
Sleaford
Lincolnshire NG34 7ES
Tel: 01529 303233.

The Alexander technique

Frederick Alexander (1869–1955) was an Australian actor; a lot of his work consisted of reciting – literally standing on a stage in front of an audience and reciting poems and stories. At the beginning of the twentieth century, Alexander experienced problems with his voice, which kept failing, threatening to ruin his career. He started to watch himself in a mirror, wondering how it was that his vocal cords kept drying up and his ability to project his voice diminished.

In fact, Alexander's study of himself covered a number of years, but he soon noticed that through tensing his muscles and changing his posture as he spoke, he was actually inhibiting his vocal muscles. In short, he was causing his own voice to fail by muscular tension.

Alexander reasoned that if, through postural error, he was the cause of his own difficulty, it followed that if he could learn to 're-balance' his body, then he could heal himself. And this is what he did. In 1904 his technique was introduced into Britain and over the years it has acquired many followers, from George Bernard Shaw to Anthea Turner. The reason why Alexander technique is not more widely taught is primarily because of cost; Alexander himself would only work on a one-to-one basis with clients, and because of his own celebrity he tended to recruit clients from among the rich and famous, principally actors, dancers and musicians. (Most drama and music schools include Alexander work in the curriculum as a matter of course.) Even today the majority of Alexander work is done in private sessions which can cost anything from £10-£50 depending on such factors as the area and the experience of the teacher. Some teachers, in an effort to introduce the technique to a wider audience, now hold classes throughout the country and these are a useful starting point; but if you can afford it, private classes with a recommended teacher are the best way.

In essence, the Alexander technique seeks to return the body to the state of balance enjoyed by small children (before hours hunched over a school desk or in front of a computer have distorted their natural equilibrium) and animals. Alexander himself was a keen horseman, and loved to watch horses move: seemingly without effort, all parts moving in a graceful whole, with no apparent tension or 'pull' anywhere.

In Alexander's phrase, we spend our lives 'armouring' ourselves. It is as if we are permanently tensed to ward off imaginary blows, clenching our muscles for fight or flight. This is the body's reaction to our noisy and stressful environment or to life events. If you sit on a bus or train and watch people in the street, you will immediately see how tense people seem, even when they are doing something as ordinary as walking down a street or waiting in a queue. It is as if the mere act of being alive takes a great deal of effort as indeed, in our society, it can do. The aim of Alexander technique is to unlearn armouring, and to release the body into a natural state of alertness.

A qualified teacher will, in effect, re-teach the pupil how to sit, stand, walk and move with the minimum of effort and in such a way that the body is moving as a whole and not as an assembly of tense, and separated, parts. In addition, a teacher spends time working with the pupil lying supine on a couch or on the floor, gently manipulating and re-aligning the body, inducing deep relaxation and a sense of wellbeing.

A key part of the practice of the technique – and something that students are recommended to do on their own at home, ideally for at least two 20-minute periods a day – is the semi-supine position. From a standing position, lower yourself to the floor and lie with legs raised, feet not too close to the buttocks, the hands placed gently on the abdomen and the elbows out. The head rests on a pile of 2-3 paperback books. A teacher will show you how to get in to and out of this position without jarring or stressing the body, and it is necessary to follow this advice in order to get the maximum benefit from the exercise. Once semi-supine, the aim is to consciously relax and stretch each body part by mental but not physical effort. When we are walking, standing or sitting 'normally' the spongy cushions of the vertebrae are crushed by the force of gravity. In adopting this position, the back relaxes and the vertebrae are 'released' from the tension of keeping us upright.

Students of Alexander technique report an enormous sense of physical wellbeing; it is also not unusual for people to feel they have grown taller in inches! This is not so, of course, but because the vertebrae are less crushed and the whole body more supple and relaxed, people do seem to be taller.

Some people – actors and performers have already been mentioned – study the technique as a means of improving their posture and acquiring physical grace. Others come to teachers because of back problems, respiratory problems or other physical ailments. Tension and distress can be quite literally absorbed and held by the body's tissues, and manifest themselves in a variety of ways. It's not uncommon for people to think they have 'neck trouble' or 'back trouble'; they do not in fact have a skeletal or orthopaedic problem, just an accumulation and manifestation of stress in those areas.

Further Reading

F. M. Alexander, *The Use of the Self.* Gollancz

Michael Gelb, *Body Learning.* Aurum Press

Glen Park, *The Art of Changing.* Ashgrove

For a list of qualified teachers, contact:
The Society of Teachers of the Alexander
Technique
20 London House
266 Fulham Road
London SW10 9EL
Tel: 0171 351 0828

Aromatherapy

The physical relaxation and sense of wellbeing afforded by massage has gained in popularity over recent years, and no variety is more popular than aromatherapy. Soothing and stroking are, as we saw in the section on transactional analysis, essential for life and growth. The first thing a mother cat or dog does with her litter is to lick them all over with her tongue: this vigorous licking doesn't just clean the pup or kitten, but stimulates their appetite and so indirectly keeps them alive.

If we're fortunate enough to have mothers who are physically affectionate, the stroking, soothing and caressing we receive as babies and children will remain with us as a positive childhood memory (even if an unconscious memory). The way a gentle mother will stroke the back and neck of a crying child is a soothing act of love we may never again experience, unless we are fortunate in our personal relationships as adults.

The combination of a relaxing massage with the use of aromatherapy oils combines two of the most potent senses: touch and smell.

The use of aromatic oils for healing has been known and practised for thousands of years. The Bible mentions the use of oils for embalming and for cleaning wounds, and in the Middle Ages European knights who had been on Crusades in the Middle East brought back a knowledge of oils with them.

For thousands of years medicines were derived from the plants growing wild in hedgerows, or cultivated in gardens, and although some were especially skilled in their use, having made a study of herbal medicine, it was a knowledge widely available to all through word of mouth, passed down from generation to generation.

During the eighteenth and nineteenth centuries chemical compounds began to replace plants in medicine, a substitution that was virtually complete by the twentieth century. It's worth remembering, however, that many medicinal plants, such as quinine, morphine, St John's Wort and atropine, have formed the basis for synthetic compounds. (St John's Wort or hypericum is a naturally occurring form of the substance used in the anti-depressant drug Prozac.)

Modern aromatherapy is generally said to have begun with a French perfume chemist called René Gattefosse. One day he accidentally burnt his hand in his laboratory and coated the wound with oil of lavender; he noticed how quickly the burn healed, and this led him to experiment further with medicinal oils. In 1928 he published a book which used the word 'aromatherapie' for the first time, but it was not until the 1980s that its practice gained popularity in Britain.

There are around 40 essential oils available, but fewer in regular use. They are now widely available from health-food stores and even chain-store chemists such as Boots routinely stock them. It is vital to stress, however, that essential oils are not just 'nice smellies' for the bath. They are potent and have a powerful effect (the basic principle is, after all, that the therapeutic oils are inhaled through the nose and therefore enter the body very close to the brain) and some of them, such as peppermint or Roman chamomile, should not be used if pregnant.

The oils may be diluted in the bath, or inhaled from a bowl of hot (not boiling) water. If you have access to a trained aromatherapist, a professional massage is extremely beneficial, especially as an introduction to aromatherapy. Of course you can also get a friend or partner to give you a massage at home – this may have the added benefit of your being in a favoured environment, but massage is a skill and this only really works if your friend or partner is good at it! A good masseur should make you feel that you are a lump of dough being skilfully prepared for the oven; a good massage is firm but gentle, methodical and rhythmic with a variety of purposeful strokes. There's nothing less conducive to inner calm than being dabbed at as if you were a door of wet paint, or feeling as if your partner is attempting to resuscitate the victim of a near drowning.

Further Reading

Julia Lawless, *The Complete Illustrated Guide to Aromatherapy.* Element

Robert Tisserand, *The Art of Aromatherapy.*

Daniel

To find a qualified practitioner, contact:
The Aromatherapy Organisations Council
P O Box 355
Croydon
Surrey CR9 2QP
Tel: 0181 2517912

Reading

We live in an information age, but often that information is often presented to us in a noisy way which invites us to be passive – we watch films or TV, or flick through magazines, while surfing the Internet is more often than not just the electronic version of flicking through a magazine.

If you're not in the habit of setting aside some personal time for reading, it's an excellent habit to develop. For one thing, you need to be quiet, in a still environment, and shutting out the noise and chaos of modern life brings instant benefits (although plenty of people manage to do their reading on the bus or the train!) Too often we walk in through the door and instantly turn on TV, radio, or music – sometimes all three. It's as if we can't be alone with our thoughts. Reading encourages us to focus, and lengthens the attention span: the more you learn and absorb, the more you are able to. The mind, as someone once said, is actually a muscle: the more you use it, the tougher it becomes. A mind with nothing more challenging to focus on than the instructions on a packet of soup rapidly becomes flabby and stale.

What to read? There never has been a time when so many books were published annually; fortunately for readers, publishers' eagerness to keep publishing seems undiminished, and few people could walk around one of the larger bookstores and not find something to interest them.

For those exploring the inner self, there are so many books of wisdom written over the centuries that the only trouble would be in knowing where to start. But it's not necessary to 'learn' from books in this fashion; good fiction can teach us as much about self-discovery as any non-fiction title.

Write your way to wisdom

Keep a diary, Mae West famously advised, and one day it will keep you. While few of us would actually want our diaries to be published – indeed, the whole idea of a diary is privacy and confidentiality – the value of putting our thoughts, feelings and expressions on paper can hardly be underestimated.

Writing is a very powerful form of therapy. On paper, we can be utterly honest. We are very seldom completely frank when talking to friends or family – for one thing, we don't want to hurt people's feelings, and the urge to present ourselves in a good light is both universal and understandable. Even when talking to a psychotherapist there can be an urge to conceal a little, to skew the image just a little. But on paper we are utterly free to let it all pour out: anger, hate, love, jealousy, pride, sorrow, regret, remorse. Someone once said that only in his diary could he put the words 'I'm sorry' and give expression to the deep regret he felt about certain events in his life; in all other areas of his life he felt the need to maintain a front.

We may not know what we truly feel about a person or an event until we begin to write about it; it's as if the act of writing, of a hand moving across a page, is a direct link with our unconscious.

What you write can be in the form of notes, or jottings, or a journal in which you record events of your day you want to remember. Some people have found it helpful to write letters to other people – letters which are never posted, but afterwards hidden away or destroyed. This is a valuable technique when people are trying to resolve old family issues, for instance, or deal with unfinished business in old relationships. Some people feel they can't move on until they've had an opportunity to put into words exactly how they feel about a particular person or situation, but realise that actually confronting that person is not the best course of action – for one thing, old emotions may be unhelpfully rekindled; for another, the person you're confronting in print may have died, or be unable to understand your point of view. This is particularly true of the generation gap, where an adult child may feel he or she has a particular grievance with a parent – who would be very distressed to read such criticisms and complaints, but powerless to deal with them.

Keeping a diary or journal does not have to be exclusively (or indeed at all) in written form. 'A Book of Myself' could be a personal record of anything and everything that is special or meaningful to you, expressing aspects of your personality: letters from others that you have kept, drawings, cuttings from papers or magazines, poems, cartoons, lists of things you enjoy doing, pictures or photos of favourite places or people – any or all of these can be included.

Some people are naturally gifted at drawing or sketching, others are not but still find it a therapeutic means of self-expression to 'play' with colours, paints, shapes, bits of stick-on glitter or transparencies. Nobody has to see this or even know that you are doing it; the point is not to make 'art' but to enjoy the moment and see what you produce.

It's a point often made that playing, which is so important in the growth and development of children, stops when we grow up. Why – when it is still so enjoyable, and brings such liberating benefits to the spirit? Get a box and fill it with crayons, chalks, glitter, glue, coloured paper, tissue paper and shapes – anything you like. Keep it for play-time, and have fun!

Further Reading
Louise de Salvo, *Writing as a Way of Healing*. The Women's Press

Expanding the mind

At the beginning of this book, I said that the whole we call the 'self' is made up of three elements: mind, body, spirit. We've talked about body and spirit, but not so much about mind in the conventional sense – that is, our intellectual capacity.

The mind is a mysterious region, a computer, a filing cabinet, a library, and a powerhouse, to name but a few of its functions. The 80s and 90s saw a resurgence of interest in things of the spirit, as evidenced by the enormous growth of interest in New Age issues; equally, the importance of health and exercise gained a new significance, and came to be more widely appreciated and understood.

But the world of the mind seems to have been ignored. There are a number of reasons. One is that we traditionally think of education as a tool; you go to school to be educated in order to get a job. But once you've passed your exams and left school, been to university or trained for a job, education becomes redundant – having served its purpose (to make you employable) you have no further need of it.

In British culture at least, there is also a certain sniffiness about 'brains'. The class egghead tends to be either bullied or ignored, and often both alternately. It's not 'done' to be seen as clever, one reason being that intellect and warmth of character are seen as mutually exclusive. If you are brainy or studious, it seems somehow to follow that you cannot also be kind-hearted, loving and generous. Academics – those who work and teach in universities and therefore make a living out of being brainy – tend to be viewed with suspicion as people who cannot really know what the real world is like.

Before we go any further, I'd like to make two things clear. The word education comes from the Latin meaning 'to draw out', meaning that a person is developed or drawn out by the process of education. I'm trying to use education in the very broadest sense of learning things, of nourishing and developing the mind, rather than in the very narrow sense of studying for exams. The second point is that learning and education should be about fulfilling individual potential, rather than striving for one uniform ideal. If everyone went to Oxford to read nuclear physics, there would be nobody left to be a plumber, or a musician, or make cars, or dig the road up. That does not, however, mean to say that someone who makes their living as a plumber or musician cannot be interested in nuclear physics.

That's another misconception about education: that it is only to do with your job. If you go to university and study engineering, for example, then there seems to be an unwritten rule that you are only interested in engineering and things mechanical, logical, machine-made. Yet there is no reason at all why a person who works all their lives as an engineer should not also play the piano, study Spanish, enjoy cooking and read all the novels of Jane Austen.

In that historical period we call the Renaissance, which flowered more brilliantly in Italy than anywhere else, a man was deemed complete because of the wide range of his interests and occupations. What we now call the ideal Renaissance man (and, given the time, they nearly all were men) was a sportsman, an athlete, a linguist, a politician, a musician – a man interested in culture as well as science, art as well as mechanics.

Even if we still view the Renaissance man as an ideal, we tend to view the reality with suspicion. Somebody commented recently that it was outrageous for a politician (in this case it may have been Mrs Thatcher) to boast that she 'never read fiction at all', as if reading a book was somehow a frivolous waste of time. It is certainly true that readers should be selective, but good fiction is an enriching thing from which we learn and our lives are enhanced. The great Victorian prime minister Disraeli would have had no patience with such an attitude: as well as being a prime minister, he was also a successful novelist.

It certainly seems to be true that as we grow older and focus more and more on our working lives and private commitments that our interests can get narrower and narrower, until for many life consists of a span of activities which goes: work – home – TV, with perhaps some shopping and a bit of sport at the weekend.

The mind is a muscle: the more you use it,

the better it is. The more you learn, the more you can learn. Much is heard now about 'multi-skilling' and in essence what this means is that the more skills and talents we can acquire, the better our chances of being employed throughout our working lives.

More and more people are finding themselves not only choosing to change their careers once or twice in their working lives, but having to. It makes sense, therefore, not to limit your options, and to keep on learning throughout your life.

That learning, however, should not be a drudgery and, as I said above, you should not feel that the only valid type of learning is that which is directly connected with an employment opportunity. And it may be – who knows when a study of calligraphy or pottery or French or wine-tasting or the history of Europe may come in useful for employment purposes (opening a restaurant in France, perhaps?)

It can be hard to find the time to enrol for courses and attend classes. It is tough to come home after a hard day at the office and face the thought of going out again to do something else. But it's only the initial effort that is a chore; most people have the experience of finding a new activity so absorbing and interesting that they feel more truly refreshed and rested than if they had spent the time in front of the TV.

Meditation

Nearly all the major religions have a tradition of meditation. The dictionary defines it as: 'To consider thoughtfully...deeply, reflect upon; to engage in contemplation'. It is a process akin to prayer, but whereas the object of prayer is to engage in a dialogue with God, the purpose of meditation may be said to be a dialogue with oneself. In fact, in some traditions the point is not to engage in anything at all, but to seek to empty the mind of all conscious thought.

There are some popular misconceptions about meditation. One is that it means going into some hypnotic trance and somehow (literally) taking leave of one's senses. People are alarmed into thinking it somehow involves a loss of control. Whereas a trance-like state may be true of some Indian mystics, this is not what the ordinary meditator seeks to achieve. In fact meditation is very much about focusing on the here and now, and rather than losing control the meditator seeks to be very much in touch with his own mind and body. Another misconception is that it is always about religion:

it isn't, and a majority of books and tapes now available teach a secular, non-religious meditation.

Of course, sitting calmly and (apparently) doing nothing is a very un-British thing to do! We live in a macho culture which feigns to mock anything 'airy fairy' or mystical. Unfortunately, there are still many circumstances where a casual remark about the benefits of meditation is likely to invite sniggers at best, at worst clear the room. Such responses are born of ignorance and, very possibly, fear. Many people are quite content to live on the surface of life, not looking too deeply into their own motives, actions and meanings. Many are genuinely afraid to be alone and quiet, even for a few moments.

When the body is quiet and calm, the mind seeks to rest: this is not the same as sleep or inactivity but rest in the sense of freedom from distraction, worries, irritations. In that calm inner space, we communicate most truly with ourselves. It is, in the truest sense of the word, a means of re-freshing ourselves.

Many traditions of meditation involve the

repetition of a word or saying, called a mantra. The repetition of this mantra (whether aloud, or in one's head) has the effect of calming, of focusing, and is often an affirmation too (a positive saying that subliminally influences the mind for the good). To some, the word chosen for the mantra is of great significance: the name of God or Jesus, for instance, to a Christian, whereas in the Buddhist tradition the mantra may evoke qualities such as compassion, humility or peace. Others say the choice of word is irrelevant, the point is that the mantra assists in helping us to focus on the process of meditation.

Other secular forms of meditation suggest that the meditator does a visualisation exercise (a walk in the mind) while sitting in tranquillity.

Transcendental meditation came to prominence in the 1960s when its chief proponent, the Maharishi Mahesh Yogi, taught the technique to the Beatles. Since then, TM has gained in popularity all over the world and has been of benefit to thousands of people. It is important to emphasise that TM is not a religion, but it does need to be taught by a qualified instructor. In essence it is no different from any other type of meditation: the meditator repeats a mantra over and over again for a period of about 20 minutes, achieving a state of 'alert restfulness'. Many doctors practice TM, and independent studies have confirmed its beneficial effects in reducing stress and increasing a sense of wellbeing.

What many have found off-putting about TM, however, is precisely the fact that it must be taught (and the technique regularly checked) by an accredited TM instructor and that this can be very expensive. The cost involved will exclude many from learning it, and this tends to bolster the image of TM as some kind of exclusive club, which is a pity.

Quite apart from TM, it is possible to be taught the techniques of meditation. Some Buddhist centres, for example, hold short introductory courses. Others prefer to learn from books or tapes, and some books are listed below.

The prerequisites for any form of meditation are that you must have a certain block of time which is completely yours. Go into a room where you will not be disturbed. If you live alone, switch the answerphone on and close the curtains if neighbours are likely to see you. Shut your cat or dog in another room – pets for some reason are immediately drawn to a person sitting still on the floor in meditation! If you live with other people, you should probably explain what you are going to do and ask to be left alone for the period of time that you are in another room with the door closed. Just saying 'I want to be left alone for 10 minutes' usually results in kind enquiries as to whether you are all right, and would a cup of tea make you feel better?

Sit on the floor if that's comfortable for you, or on a straight-backed chair. The typical image of a meditator is of someone cross-legged in the lotus position, but for many people this is very uncomfortable and not a position that can be maintained for long. The point is to be comfortable and relaxed, but not to be slouched or so cosy that you fall asleep. For a majority of people, sitting upright in a chair, with hands in your lap and feet on the floor, is sustainable.

Wear comfortable clothes, loosen or remove any ties or restrictive clothing, and take off your shoes. Feel the floor or carpet beneath your toes. Be warm – nobody can sit focusing on their meditation if they are actually shivering with cold.

Some meditate with eyes closed, some like to keep their eyes open and focus on some object -- a glowing candle, for instance, or a crystal.

Begin by consciously relaxing your body: begin with your toes, focus on them, wriggle them perhaps, and relax them. Then think of your feet, stretch them perhaps, wriggle them, think of the muscles in each part of the foot, and relax them. Work up your body, thinking in turn of each limb and part of it – including mouth, eyes, ears and face – and think of that part of your body shedding tension and relaxing. Imagine a sponge squeezing out water and bouncing back into its shape. Imagine tension as a heavy damp coat on your shoulders, and shrug it off.

There are as many visualisation exercises as the imagination can find, but here is one to start you off:

Think of a place very special to you. It may be a real place, somewhere you have been on holiday perhaps, or a corner of your garden. It may be an imaginary place, somewhere described in a book. It may be a mountain, a beach, a wood, a garden, a country lane. You are walking to reach that place, slowly and calmly looking at all the things you see in the last part of your journey. Listen to the birds in the trees, or maybe the sound of waves on the shore. Listen in turn to each of the sounds you can hear in this place. Then focus on the smell of the place: herbs growing on a hillside in the sun, perhaps, or the pungent salty smell of the sea. Perhaps it's raining, and the rain is soft and damp on your face, caressing, moist. Perhaps the sun is warming your skin, you can feel its rays on your arms, your back, your face. Slowly you come into this magical, special place. You are safe here; it is a place friendly to you, no harm can come to you. You are strong here, and at peace. Breathe the air, breathe deeply, breathe in the clean shining air and then let your breath go. Keep breathing deeply while you listen, again, to each sound in turn. Spend some time in this place, and then slowly turn to go. There is no need to hurry. Slowly take yourself back to the place you started from, and pause. When you feel ready to, slowly open your eyes.

Further Reading

Bill Anderton, *Meditation.* Piatkus

Barry Long, *Meditation: A Foundation Course.* Barry Long Books

Jessica Macbeth, *Moon over Water.* Gateway Books

Victor N. Davich, *The Best Guide to Meditation.* Renaissance Books

Diana Brueton, *Discovering Meditation.* How To Books

To find out about learning TM, telephone: *0990 143 733.*

Dream interpretation

Paying attention to your dreams is an important tool in the journey of the self.

Ancient civilisations valued dreams as insights or messages sent from the gods and prized the men who could interpret them. In the Bible, you'll remember that Joseph (he of the Coat of Many Colours) made a successful career out of dream interpretation. Often people felt that dreams foretold the future, and interpreted them literally, and many dreams are still recorded in which people feel future events have been predicted. This is called precognition; few, however, have the experience of John Williams in 1933. Williams was a Quaker, and as such was not a betting man -the idea of gambling was against his principles. Because of this, Williams took no interest in racing, but on Derby Day he dreamed that he was listening to the radio and heard the names of the two winners announced. He was puzzled by this dream – considering he had no interest in the subject matter – and made a note of it, finding to his astonishment that when the race was actually won he had dreamt the names of the winner and the runner-up.

Today, dreams are viewed as messages from our own unconscious rather than from external sources like the gods. One of the founding fathers of psychoanalysis, Carl Gustav Jung, wrote much about the importance of dreams. He wrote down the dreams he remembered and asked his patients to recount their dreams to him; he felt this was a key to understanding their deepest fears and feelings.

We all dream – even animals do – but of course we seldom remember what we dream. We are aware of having had vivid and colourful experiences, which fade as we wake. The theory is that this is because they have 'worked'.

Dreams are a direct link with our unconscious minds. In our waking lives, the brain acts as a powerful filter, sorting out all that information that is not useful to us as we go about our daily lives – often, it also suppresses that which is painful, or that which we do not choose to scrutinise too closely. Though usually we do so unconsciously, we are very good at 'conning' ourselves, often for reasons of pure survival. The man who is deeply unhappy in his marriage, for instance, may block out such thoughts because in admitting the truth he would be forced to act, and in some part of his being he has decided that such action would cause too many repercussions, and he shrinks from it.

When we dream, the lid comes off the unconscious. That's why the world of our dreams so often seems crazy or irrational – it's not a world that has to obey the logic or the rules of cold reality.

Freud used a technique called free association in the interpretation of dreams, and many other psychoanalysts still do. The technique is rather like following a ball of string to its source; a patient recounts a dream in which, for example, in which a horse features as an important image. The analyst asks the client to clear his mind and say, quickly and without thought, what images come in his mind connected with horses. If the point of the dream is, for example, something connected with the dreamer's father, it may be that the repetition of every word he associates with horse eventually leads to the 'answer'.

As we sleep (and remember we spend roughly a third of our lives doing this), our dreams work on the problems and issues of the day. Our unconscious, which during the day has been kept under control like a dog on a leash, is freed to roam at will. And so all our real concerns are turned and tossed about, and our brains work busily at ordering and sorting our experience, storing it in the unconscious like files in a computer.

When a problem is 'sorted', or neatly 'filed', the dream has done its work. There is no purpose in our remembering it. When we remember a dream, it is because the issue the dream represents has not been resolved; the dream is telling us to pay attention, to look at our lives, to examine the issue.

Everyone has an intensely personal language of dreams. There are many books available on interpreting the language of dreams and unfortunately a few of them are very silly; it is not true, for instance (as I read in one book) that if you dream of furniture it's because you will marry a cabinet maker who will keep you poor but happy. There are some symbols which are said to be constant: for instance, the sea or water are said to represent sexuality; a house is said to represent your own personality (with the storeys of a house representing the levels of consciousness). But each symbol needs to be tested in terms of its personal meaning for you.

For example, two people can go to a concert of a piece of classical music, or go to see the same film. For one person, the music of Mahler symbolises the triumph of hope over suffering; for the other person, Mahler is the composer of absolute, inconsolable misery. One person sees the film as a happy romantic story; the other interprets it as a cynical comment on modern morals. Both are, of course, right – they are interpreting what they see and hear from their own personal standpoint. In the second century AD an Ephesian called Artemidorus wrote a five-volume study called The Book of Dreams, which remained definitive until Freud and Jung started work in the twentieth century. Even in his day, Artemidorus noted that: 'The same dream does not always have the same meaning in each case and for each person. It can vary depending on the time and place…if we wish to interpret a dream correctly, we need to take note of whether the person…is male or female, healthy or sick, a free man or a slave, rich or poor, young or old.'

Erotic dreams, for instance, are very common. Some people feel quite embarrassed about them. But the meaning of such a dream will be very different depending on whether you are, for example, a 17-year-old boy or a 53-year-old woman.

Another analogy in dream work is that of the cryptic crossword clue. I've often looked at such clues for ages, puzzling over them; they seem impenetrable. The next day I look at the printed answer and say 'of course!' It may not have been particularly difficult or beyond my scope – just that my brain wasn't looking at it from the right angle.

It takes time to learn to work with your dreams. To start with, keep a dream diary. Have a scrap of paper and a pen by your bedside; you can fumble for them as you wake and jot down the essentials of what you remember in note form ('rain – Mother – fog – boss came in wearing pyjamas and told me not to forget the post'). Then, when you first get up, sit with a cup of tea or coffee and write up your jottings in a notebook. The key thing is to write down exactly what you remember, and don't try to tidy up or interpret what you recall. What you remember may seem to you to be nonsense: never mind, write it down anyway.

Remember that alcohol and certain drugs can affect the way you dream – or not. Some sleeping pills, for instance, actually inhibit the dreaming process, which means that the sleep you do have is not fully refreshing; because they curb a natural process, coming off them can lead to a sort of rebound effect, whereby you experience panic attacks, nightmares and other unpleasant side effects. If you need sleeping pills, talk to your doctor about these likely side effects and what you can do to diminish them. There is some truth, apparently, in the old wives' tale that cheese and heavy meals before can lead (not only to indigestion) but also to disturbed sleep and nightmares. Heavy alcohol consumption has been implicated in panic attacks and nightmares, but it is now thought that this is more likely to happen when the dreamer is coming off alcohol.

Fritz Perls, the founder of gestalt therapy, advised his clients to act out their dreams, as far as possible (playing all the roles themselves!) In so doing, the therapist – observing the body language, vocabulary and gestures the dreamer uses in recalling the dreams, can use these as additional aids to interpretation.

As the months pass, you will not only become better at remembering and writing down your dreams the more you practice doing so, but you will have distance from them, and see more clearly what they are saying to you. Dream interpretation has to be learned, like playing the piano.

Remember also that you may be too close to the events. As an example of this, many years ago I was in a dead-end relationship that was clearly going nowhere. And yet in my conscious, everyday mind I could not admit this. I had a series of puzzling dreams which I faithfully recorded, even though I thought they were daft. Years later, I can read those dreams and see obvious images of dead-ends everywhere: the dream was telling me how unhappy I was, and urging me to cut my losses. At the time, my conscious mind stifled the insights my dreams were trying to convey.

That is another lesson to be learned: the more we learn about ourselves and trust ourselves, the more we can learn to go with our dreams. The great psychotherapist Carl Rogers used to say: 'The facts are friendly'. Our dreams are facts, our unconscious mind is a fact – it is a part of us, and it is friendly. There are no parts of our own selves that we should fear, or shy away from. I'm on my side, is the message.

There are many therapists – often trained in the methods of Carl Jung – who use dream interpretation in their work. If you really start to feel that your dreams are trying to speak to you, it is worth seeking out such a person to work with. The detached insight of another person is often invaluable.

Further Reading
Gayle Delaney, *All About Dreams*. HarperSan Francisco
Betty Bethards, *The Dream Book*. Element

Michele Simmons and Chris McLaughlin, *Dream Interpretation: A Beginner's Guide*. Headway

Death: the final frontier

In Victorian times, sex was the great taboo which could never be mentioned. Today, it seems, we seldom talk about anything else. Instead, it is death which has become the great taboo. Start to talk about it, and people look away, shift their gaze and hurriedly change the subject.

We all die, to state the obvious. Rich, famous, celebrated, photographed, loved, needed – none of this matters in the end. It comes by accident or through illness – hopefully it comes peacefully and in a ripe old age – but come it will. It's perhaps not an exaggeration to imagine that when Diana Princess of Wales died it was the first time many people had come close to the death of someone they loved. That someone so visible, so photographed, so vibrant, so alive, should suddenly be no more seemed shocking and incomprehensible.

In searching to find ourselves, in seeking a knowledge of self, we have to face and embrace the fact that one day we will die: our selves as we now experience them will cease to be. For the person of faith, of course, this is not necessarily so, and the question of what happens after death and how to prepare for it occupies a large part of the teachings of the great religions. The one incontrovertible fact of our lives is the most difficult to face, but in the search for ourselves, we cannot be truly human and mature if we cannot look death in the face.

If we're fortunate, we will be well into adulthood before losing anyone we know or love. It is almost a marker of maturity, of the passage of time, that we count it in terms of those who have gone before us. The death of a parent is a particularly poignant rite of passage. They were there before we were: because of them, I am. In losing a parent, we lose a most significant part of ourselves, and for many people it is the first real intimation of mortality. One day, we think, this will be me. Just as I now stand at my mother's grave and remember her cuddling me, or picking up my Lego, or scolding me for being naughty, or cooking Sunday lunch, so one day will my children stand at my grave and think of me.

Premature deaths, through illness, violence,

accident or suicide, enrage us as an abuse of the natural order. The elderly can be mourned with honour and a sense of 'they'd had their life'; to bury someone young and with so much still to look forward to – as for example the television presenter Jill Dando – is a terrifying reminder of how frail this thing called life is. It can be rubbed out in an unfair instant, and those who are left will never be the same.

It may seem strange in a book that encourages a focus on life to mention death. But in exploring our inner selves, how we feel about life cannot be entirely separated from how we feel about death. Life is all too short and should be cherished and enriched as much as we can; we must also hope to find the grace and maturity to meet that final end when it comes, both for ourselves and those whom we love.

Further Reading

Ruth Picardie, *Before I say Goodbye*. Penguin

Liz Tilberis, *No Time to Die*. Weidenfield & Nicolson

Dinah Seibert et al, *Are you Sad too? Helping children deal with loss and death*. ETR

Association Paperback

Jeroid O'Neil Roussell, *Dealing with Grief,
Theirs and Ours*. Alba House

CRUSE, the counselling organisation for the
bereaved, can be contacted at:
Cruse House
126 Sheen Road
Richmond
Surrey TW9 1UR
Tel: 0181 332 7227

CHAPTER 5
FAMILY HISTORY

Tracing our roots

Why should an exploration of the inner self encompass our family history?

The more we find out about ourselves, the more we need to connect with what is around us. 'Only connect' in a therapeutic sense means the need to connect up our private pasts with our present; but as human beings we don't exist in isolation. We are connected by birth to our families, our ancestors, and by ties of blood and history to our race, our country, our heritage.

It seems to be a tendency that the older we get, the more interested we are in family history. This is a shame; often those who could tell us most have by this time died, and when we were small children listening to Granny or Grandpa with their endless reminiscences was often tedious for active young bodies.

A hundred years ago, populations were hardly mobile and family life was stable. If you were born in a village in Dorset in 1890, the chances are that your parents and grandparents were, too – or at least, not too far away. You may well have grown up in the same house that your father grew up in. If you wanted to know who your great-grandfather was, he was probably buried in the churchyard and you passed his headstone every Sunday morning. In agricultural communities, professions tended to be handed on in families too. If your father was a blacksmith or a dairyman or a joiner, then the chances were that you would follow the same trade too.

That way of life had begun to fragment earlier, of course, with the Industrial Revolution in the late eighteenth and early nineteenth centuries. Then the great cities grew up, with their factory chimneys belching poisonous smoke, offering however employment to the masses whom the land could no longer support. And if one city or factory could no longer offer you work, then you could load your belongings on to a cart as Jude Fawley did in Thomas

Hardy's novel, and move on.

The pace of life changed more slowly in the countryside, but change it did and the lives our grandparents lived before the Second World War would seem as foreign to us now as if they were Chinese peasants working in a state commune.

It would seem strange to earlier generations that we can often know nothing about even our grandparents' generation, but this is becoming increasingly true. I will never even see the house in which my father grew up – indeed, it probably no longer exists. The fragmentation of family life that comes with divorce and remarriage accelerates the rate at which we lose touch with our roots, who we are, where we come from, what our ancestors did. When a marriage breaks down and people move away from each other, children lose their grandparents as well, they lose great-aunts and uncles, they lose links with a past that one day they may want to rekindle.

The number of books on the market to do with genealogy and tracing family history is evidence of a growing interest in gathering information about our own actual family tree. A selection of these is listed at the end of this section.

Two notes of caution: many often embark on a study of their family history hoping to unearth glamorous or celebrated forebears; it's remarkable the number of families, for instance, who believe themselves to be descended from aristocracy or even royalty. Of course, given the sexual morals of lords of the manor and members of the royal family (in earlier times, I hasten to add) it's perfectly possible that many towns and villages throughout Britain had a baby or two whose father was not the person whose name appeared on the birth certificate, if indeed there was one. In the main, however, the long slog backwards in time will reveal only a respectable line of honest, hardworking but definitely ordinary people.

The other point is perhaps more serious. There are numerous stories of people who have, in tracing family records, uncovered secrets that may still cause distress to living persons. Until very recently, for instance, having a child outside marriage was a source of shame both to mother and child, and members of your family of an older generation may be unwilling to have such things revealed. There will also be a good number of babies born less than nine months after a wedding, and sensitivity is needed in such cases. Just because something happened 50 years ago does not mean the emotions connected with it are not still fresh to those involved.

Remember that up until the 1960s or even later 'illegitimate' babies were a secret, and a majority of such babies were put up for adoption. This was considered the only sensible solution for mother and child. It stands to reason, therefore, that there must be a number of people now living – children who are now in their 30s or 40s, women in their 50s or 60s – who represent the two halves of a mother-and-child relationship severed at birth. From time to time the papers will report the story of a famous person (the politician Clare Short and the actress Pauline Collins spring to mind) who gave up a child for adoption in those days, and the poignancy of their stories makes painful reading.

It is also true that embarking on the trail of family history is how many people discover for the first time that either they or other family members have been adopted. It is only in the comparatively recent past that child psychologists and adoption agencies have actively encouraged parents to be truthful with their adopted children about their origins. Openness and frankness ('we chose you, we didn't just have you, we wanted you especially') can avoid the traumas suffered by many adopted children in later life. Adoption is dealt with in a separate section, but suffice it to say here that embarking on a study of your family history can be a lot of fun and absolutely fascinating; but it's wise to be prepared for any shocks that may emerge.

This increasing interest in social history, or the history of ordinary people, has been seen on a national level too. As the twentieth century closed, there were a number of television programmes on 'oral history' – that is, the memories of those born and growing up in the earlier part of the century. In listening to older folk talking about life on the land before the Second World War, or their memories of the war itself, or what life was like even earlier, was not only fascinating in itself and a way of deepening our knowledge of the world and how it has been shaped, but helped us as individuals to feel linked to that past. That, after all, is where we have come from.

Local Record offices, where the records of births, marriages and deaths are kept, have reported an enormous increase in the number of enquiries they receive from those seeking to illuminate their own personal histories, and as a result of this have become much more approachable and helpful places.

The Record Office is the obvious place to start, but family history can only be traced back one step at a time – which adds to the fascination as the mystery is unravelled slowly. You need to know where your parents were married in order to find out (if you do not know) where they were born and the births registered, and only in tracking down a copy of your grandfather's birth records will you find out where your great-grandfather hailed from, and so on.

There is now even computer software available to assist in drawing up a family tree. (See the very helpful book by Matthew and April Helm listed below.) In the old days, it was the custom to log such information in the family Bible. This Bible was a valued possession, and usually a big leather-bound book the size of a small table top. The head of the family was charged with writing in, on the blank pages, the names and dates of birth of each member of the family. It can be fascinating to look at such Bibles in local museums. The poet Robert Burns' Bible is kept in the Burns Museum in Dumfries, for example, and in it the poet's large firm writing records the dates of significance in his family. Poignantly, the date of his favourite daughter's death is also recorded, three years after her birth in 1792.

Family Bibles may be a thing of the past, but it is still worthwhile in every household to have a special album dedicated to the members of that household. In today's society, that book may contain the records of an extended family; in the case of divorce and remarriage, it may be painful to have photographs or details of a former partner, but try to think of the Family Book as a piece of history which will be cherished and looked into for generations, and not so much a personal record of pain (although future generations will understand that, too). A former wife or husband may be an individual you would rather forget completely, but if you have had a child with this person, then it is only fair that that child's child should have access to information about them.

The Family Book can be as simple as a scrapbook or as lavish as an expensively bound volume. The main thing it should contain is a family tree of the family as it exists today, with the dates of birth (and death) for every individual known. In the case of large families, you may have to decide to limit the tree to close relatives only. Only children will usually be glad to include as many cousins or other distant relatives as they can.

Other pieces of information or items which the album might include are: photographs of family members, past and present; wedding invitations; Orders of Service for weddings or funerals; locks of babies' hair; photographs of houses where family members have lived; receipts for important events (this may seem trivial now – but think how much interest we derive from a receipt for, for example, a car bought in 1961, or the wedding reception Uncle Jack paid for in 1953); important letters or telegrams.

It's important to be selective (other family archive items can be stored safely in boxes) in order to keep the book as a record – too much personal information and it is more like a diary. Remember also to include as many facts as possible, for future generations. 'Uncle Jack died 1956' is enough for those who knew him, but for those born after his death 'Uncle Jack died of pneumonia aged 49 in Withington General Hospital, having fallen ill after the village fete' will give a much more rounded and valuable picture.

Modern houses tend to be small and space is at a premium: people move around so much that keeping 'rubbish' to a minimum makes sense and may indeed be the only option. But when you next have a major clear-out, try to preserve those items personal to you and your family which future generations may thank you for. Some people, I know, never ever throw a letter away; while that may be excessive (and not practical unless you have an attic!) try to hold on to those letters which your children and grandchildren will find fascinating – letters from husbands to wives, for instance, written before they were married, or thank-you letters written by small children for Christmas presents. When those children grow up and have children of their own, the letters will be a cherished keepsake.

As people grow older, younger generations can find it hard to visualise them as 'real' people – Granny is just a white-haired old lady who finds it hard to hear what is said to her. How thrilling, then, to bring Granny's past to life with love letters written to her by Grandpa when he was away on active service in the war, for example. (Of course, everyone has the right to censor the letters they choose to keep!)

History is being made today, it's not just in the past, so it's up to us to preserve what we can of yesterday and select and save those aspects of our own lives which will give meaning to future generations.

Another good place to start is with the senior members of your family today. The writer Jung Chang, eager to hear of her mother's past life during the Chinese revolution, invested in a tape recorder which she gave to her mother, begging her to speak into it with her memories. The result was the basis for the classic Wild Swans.

Not everyone will end up with a best-seller of course, or would want to, but modern technology can help us record the past. Writing memories longhand may be laborious and impossible for the elderly, but speaking into a tape recorder or dictaphone involves little effort and can, in fact, provide a lonely elderly person with a most enjoyable and worthwhile project.

Further Reading

Mark D. Herber and John Titford, *Ancestral Trails*. Sutton

Rosemary Bigwood, Collins Pocket Reference: Tracing Scottish Ancestors. HarperCollins

Brian Loomes, *Concise Guide to Tracing your*

Ancestors. Barrie & Jenkins

Noel Currer-Biggs et al, *Debrett's Guide to Tracing your Family Tree*. Debrett)

David Hey, *The Oxford Guide to Family History*. Oxford

Matthew L. Helm and April Leigh Helm, *Genealogy Online for Dummies*. IDG

Adoption

For a large number of people, the search for
your inner self will be a metaphorical search.
The answer to the question 'Who am I?' can be
answered only in terms of your spiritual,
emotional, intellectual life.

But there are those for whom the question
'Who am I?' has a very real and special meaning
– people adopted at birth or as young children,
or children who never were adopted but have
grown up instead in a variety of institutions
and foster homes.

Our parents are our starting point in life.
Through them, we came into the world, and in
a sense we always define ourselves by our
parents. Perhaps more importantly, so does
society. How often do you read in the papers
that so-and-so was 'the son of a plumber' or 'a
doctor's daughter from Surrey'? Britain (still)
tends to be a class-conscious culture; as a
nation we have a tendency to put people into
categories according to the status held by their
parents. We have an exaggerated respect for
wealth and 'breeding'; people from working-

class backgrounds who 'make good' have often struggled against enormous barriers of snobbery and prejudice to get where they are, though seldom get the admiration they deserve.

Parents may be are the beginning point, but the rest of it is up to us. The whole dream of American society is based on the 'log cabin to White House' story, referring to Abraham Lincoln and his rise to the presidency from very humble beginnings. It is part of the strength and vibrancy of the United States that as a nation it has this encouraging philosophy; it doesn't matter where you come from, what matters is who you are and where you are going.

Detractors of British culture have often (with not a little justification) pointed out that our national attitude tends to be more gruding and resentful. In America, if you drive a luxury car, people say: 'Wow! Great! Guess if I get to be as successful as you, I can have one of these'. Typically, Britons would sneer: 'Who does he think he is? He's only a bloody shopkeeper's [or whatever] son'.

The urge to know who your natural parents were is both natural and overwhelming.

In an earlier section, I described the prevailing picture before the 1960s. Pregnancy outside marriage was a scandal to be kept as a shameful secret as long as possible. As has been famously remarked, sex was not invented in 1963, and prior to 1963 people behaved much as they always have done throughout the centuries. What made all the difference was, of course, the invention of the contraception pill (which became freely available during the 1960s) and the legalisation of abortion in 1967. Before the 1960s, a woman who found herself pregnant but without a husband had three choices: one was to get married quickly, always assuming that her partner was willing (or known, or able to marry her); another was to risk her own life by having an illegal backstreet abortion – such procedures, being illegal, were by their very nature performed by sleazy (often unqualified) individuals in conditions often dangerously insanitary and almost always mercilessly shabby; the third was to arrange for the baby to be removed from the mother immediately at birth and given up for adoption. Society put enormous pressure on these unmarried pregnant women – often no more than girls, very young, very vulnerable and very much alone – to give their babies up, and without strong family or financial support it would be virtually impossible for a girl to go ahead with her pregnancy alone and rear the baby as a single mother.

The fate of the babies was to find themselves, in the vast majority of cases, adopted into loving homes where they were very much wanted. Nobody, after all, adopts a child by accident. Adoption law in Britain has been criticised for its rigidity – particularly in recent years when it has militated against single parents or gay couples adopting children – but in its defence one can only say that the aim of the law has been to put the child's safety and wellbeing first, as is only right (even if it's time to rethink what that may mean).

The fate of the mothers, though, must arouse compassion. The baby was handed over to the adoptive parents with little or no information passed on about the natural mother; the mother herself had no right to know where her child had gone. Contact was lost altogether. There must be many women today carrying the tragic secret of a child they have never seen or known. It is only in the past 20 years, with a growing awareness of the emotional ties of birth and mothering, that concern for the psychological effects of adoption have been explored.

In 1975, the UK law changed to allow those who had been adopted to have access to their original birth certificates. This change set many people off on the search to find out who they really were, and in many cases these searches involved enormous difficulty and emotional trauma.

In the first place, the trail had often gone cold. Although a parent's name (if known, in the case of the father) must be recorded on the birth certificate, there is no way of knowing where that person is now, unless they have somehow kept in contact through mutual sources. Given the social condemnation surrounding illegitimate births, many women who gave up their babies for adoption will have 'disappeared' without trace, moved to another city, married, changed their names, or be otherwise untraceable. Many adopted children have spent literally months and years going through telephone directories, contacting local authorities, hospitals, adoption agencies, placing advertisements in local and national newspapers, in attempts to track down their natural parents. The organisation NORCAP (National Organisation for the Counselling of Adoptees and their Parents) was founded in 1982 to help those searching for birth parents, and to offer advice and counselling both to them and to the birth parents when found.

Those adopted before 12 November 1975 are provided with counselling as a matter of course, after taking the decision to seek their birth parents and before being shown the relevant files; great care is taken not just to hand over records without a discussion of the possible consequences. Those born and adopted after that date may choose whether or not to have counselling.

There are of course three parties involved in such a search, and all have different sources of anguish: the child, the birth parents, and the adopted parents.

The adopted parents, first of all, will need a

great deal of inner strength to support their child during his or her search. It would be only natural to feel a certain sense of rejection: after all, these people probably had their own tale of woe before they were able to adopt a child – perhaps they suffered the anguish of infertility, or lost babies through miscarriage. Whatever their story, it is certain that there is one before the moment that they were accepted by the adoption agency and 'given' their child. To bond with that child, bring him or her up, love, cherish and educate them, and then have them fired with enthusiasm and hunger to contact their 'real' parents is a situation demanding enormous maturity and love to cope with. Almost by implication, a parent that is 'real' has the advantage over one who is not – even though, as we said earlier, nobody adopts a child by accident; plenty of babies, though, are conceived by accident and not really wanted at all.

The birth parents may not, after all, want to be contacted. Even if they can be found and located, their lives may have moved on. The time of the child's birth was probably painful and unhappy, and they have no wish to be reminded of that period. A woman who has given up her child for adoption may not have told her subsequent husband and family of that earlier child, and it may be a secret she has every reason to want to keep. A child who tracks down his natural mother, only to be told that she does not wish to have any contact him, will suffer a huge sense of rejection which can only echo that earlier rejection many adopted children feel ('my real mother didn't want me.')

Rejection is one of the hardest experiences with which we have to cope because it strikes at the very core of who we are. Rejection says 'I don't want you' and this makes us feel less valid as human beings. Being rejected by a lover is survivable; most people, in the end, come to terms with that and even come to feel that they are better off without that person. A healthy ego, with sufficient self-esteem, can bounce back saying 'It's his problem, not mine, I'm OK'.

But at the very root of our personalities as human beings lies the relationship with the mother. Much of what I say applies to fathers too, but the bond may be less strong because of the physical closeness of mother and baby. It is the sine qua non of most people's existence that they have a mother who loves them unconditionally, who carried them for nine months, who gave birth to them, who nursed them as babies. It is exceptionally hard for anyone to feel that they have been rejected by their mother.

Rejection is, of course, a two-way street. Although we feel rejection as a deeply personal wound ('I am no good, I am not worth anything, I have been rejected') it says as much about the person doing the rejecting. In the case of, for example, a teenage girl who gives her baby up for adoption, she will almost certainly not have consciously rejected her child. It was just all too much for her: the anger of her parents, the shame of her family, the apparent ruin of her social life and educational hopes. Perhaps the boy she thought loved her abandoned her; almost certainly people sniggered about her behind her back. Once this whole desperately sad episode was over, all she wanted to do was pick up the pieces and forget it. Apparently cruel and rejecting behaviour is often simply a cover for an inability to cope with great pain in any other way.

The adopted child will be torn by a number of emotions. Many feel guilt at 'doing this' to their adopted parents, whom they genuinely love and have no wish to hurt. Many feel a great sense of excitement at meeting their birth mother, and subsequently feel let down: it may be that the adopted child had built up a fantasy picture of the birth parent or parents. It may be that the birth mother will prove to be warm, loving and exciting in a way that the adopted mother is not; the child may feel a lack or need within himself that he is sure the birth mother can fill. Instead, the birth mother turns out to be an ordinary person with whom the child feels no especial bond.

Some adopted children, meeting their birth parents, have reported a sense of shock at seeing the physical resemblance (which is of course missing from their relationship with their adopted parents) but at the same time not feeling any kind of instant bond or connection. Psychologists have argued the nature vs. nurture case for years – is there such a thing as a 'natural', innate mother love, or is it something developed over years through caring for your child? Do children love their parents just because they have always been there? Witness the loyalty abused and cruelly treated children still seem to show towards their undeserving parents; this might seem to argue that loving your parents is innate.

As usual, the truth is somewhere between the two. Nature arranges that there will be an instant chemical link – rather like falling in love at first sight – between mothers and babies, in order to ensure that the young are cared for and survive. In the world of nature, that bond dissolves once the young are weaned. In the human world, an even stronger bond is forged over years of caring and nurturing on the part of the mother.

At the end of this trail of discovery or loss, there is a truth from psychotherapy that is healing. Whether we search for our birth parents, or feel that our birth parents did not love and nurture us the way that we hoped, leaving us in consequence as fragmented adults trying to become whole, the truth is that we can learn to lovingly parent ourselves. In exploring our inner selves, and gaining strength and confidence from that courageous process, we become both nurturing mother and protective father to our own, unique personalities.

● NORCAP (National Organisation for the Counselling of Adoptees and their Parents) may be contacted at:

112 Church Road
Wheatley
Oxon OX33 1LU
Tel: 01865 875000

Addict Stephen Smith (Westworld)

All About Dreams Gayle Delaney (Harper San Francisco)

An Introduction to Jung's Psychology Frieda Fordham (Pelican)

Ancestral Trails Mark D. Herber and John Titford (Sutton)

Are you Sad too? Helping children deal with loss and death Dinah Seibert et al (ETR Association Paperback)

Aspects in Astrology Sue Tompkins (Element)

Astrology Carole Golder (Piatkus)

Astrology Warren Kenton (Thames and Hudson)

Astrology and Childhood Peter West (London House)

Astrology and Health Dylan Warren-Davies (Headway)

Before I say Goodbye Ruth Picardie (Penguin)

Body Learning Michael Gelb (Aurum Press)

Born to Win Muriel James and Dorothy Jongeward (Addison Wesley)

Calm Down Paul Hauck (Sheldon Press)

Collins Pocket Reference: Tracing Scottish Ancestors Rosemary Bigwood (HarperCollins)

Concise Guide to Tracing your Ancestors Brian Loomes (Barrie & Jenkins)

Dealing with Grief, Theirs and Ours Jeroid O'Neil Roussell (Alba House)

Debrett's Guide to Tracing your Family Tree Noel Currer-Biggs et al (Debrett)

Discovering Meditation Diana Brueton (How To Books)

Dream Interpretation: A Beginner's Guide Michele Simmons and Chris McLaughlin (Headway)

Freud for Beginners Richard Osborne (Writers and Readers Paperback)

Games People Play Eric Berne (Penguin)

Genealogy Online for Dummies Matthew L. Helm and April Leigh Helm (IDG)

Gestalt Self Therapy Muriel Schiffman (Wingbow)

Gestalt Therapy Frederick S Perls (Souvenir Press)

Getting off the merry-go-round Carla Perez (Impact)

Gifts Differing: Understanding Personality Types Isabel
B. Myers with Peter Myers (Davies-Black
Publishing)

Healing the Hurt Within Jan Sutton (Pathways)

Healing the Shame that Binds you John Bradshaw
(Health Communications)

Homecoming John Bradshaw (Piatkus)

I'm OK, You're OK Thomas A. Harris (Arrow)

Illustrated Light on Yoga B K S Iyengar (Thorsons)

Introduction to Type and Careers Allen L. Hammer
(Oxford Psychologists Press)

Jung for Beginners Maggie Hyde and Michael
McGuinness (Icon)

Life Lines Peter West (Foulsham)

Meditation Bill Anderton (Piatkus)

Meditation: A Foundation Course Barry Long (Barry
Long Books)

Memories, Dreams, Reflections Carl Gustav Jung

(Fontana)

Moon over Water Jessica Macbeth (Gateway Books)

No Time to Die Liz Tilberis (Weidenfield & Nicolson)

Own your own Life Richard G Abell (Bantam)

Sigmund Freud, The Interpretation of Dreams (Ed. Angela Richards; Penguin)

TA Today Ian Stewart and Vann Joines (Lifespace)

The Art of Aromatherapy Robert Tisserand (Daniel)

The Art of Changing Glen Park (Ashgrove)

The Best Guide to Meditation Victor N. Davich (Renaissance Books)

The Complete Illustrated Guide to Aromatherapy Julia Lawless (Element)

The Complete Illustrated Guide to Palmistry Peter West (Element)

The Complete Yoga Book James Hewitt (Rider)

The Drama of Being a Child Alice Miller (Virago)

The Dream Book Betty Bethards (Element)

The Effective Way to Stop Drinking Beauchamp Colclough and Elton John (Penguin)

The Essentials of Psychoanalysis Sigmund Freud

(Penguin)

The Freud Reader Peter Gay (ed.) (Penguin)

The Oxford Guide to Family History David Hey (Oxford)

The Red Book of Gestalt Gaie Houston (Rochester)

The Use of the Self F. M. Alexander (Gollancz)

Understanding Ourselves: The Uses of Therapy Joan Woodward (Macmillan)

Understanding the Twelve Steps Terence T. Gorski (Simon & Schuster)

Understanding your Personality Patricia Hodges (Sheldon Press)

Writing as a Way of Healing Louise de Salvo (The Women's Press)

Yoga for Common Ailments Dr R Monro, Dr Nagarathna and Dr Nagendra (Gaia)

Yoga for Stress Relief Swami Shivapremananda (Gaia)

Alcoholics Anonymous
Tel: 0345 697555

CAER
Rosemerryn, Lamorna,
Penzane,
Cornwall TR19 6BN
Tel: 01736 810530

CRUSE
Cruse House,
126 Sheen Road,
Richmond,
Surrey TW9 1UR
Tel: 0208 332 7227

Drinkline (information and counselling services)
Tel: 0345 320202

NORCAP (National Organisation for the Counselling
of Adoptees and their Parents)
112 Church Road,
Wheatley,
Oxon OX33 1LU
Tel: 01865 875000

Scottish Yoga Teachers Association
Frances Corr,
26 Buckingham Terrace,
Edinburgh EH4 3AE
Tel: 0131 343 3553

The Aromatherapy Organisations Council
P O Box 355,
Croydon,
Surrey CR9 2QP
Tel: 0181 2517912

The British Association for Counselling
1 Regent Place,
Rugby,
Warwickshire CV21 2PJ
Tel: 01788 578328
Email: bac@BAC.co.uk

The British Wheel of Yoga
1 Hamilton Place,
Boston Road,
Sleaford, Lincolnshire NG34 7ES
Tel: 01529 303233

The Samye Ling Centre
Eskdalemuir,
Dumfries-shire, DG13 0QL
Tel: 013873 73232

The Society of Teachers of the Alexander Technique
20 London House,
266 Fulham Road,
London SW10 9EL
Tel: 0171 351 0828

The Yoga Therapy Centre
Royal London Homeopathic Hospital
60 Great Ormond Street,
London WC1N 3HR
Tel: 0171 419 7195

TM
Tel: 0990 143 733